If you have a positive attitude then you move towards your goal keeping yourself cool even at the time of adverse situations. And if you have negativity even for small things then people around you will become your enemies. Positive attitude is a power which can make even your enemy your friend. Gandhiji had this power of positive attitude. He has developed a kind of internal light within himself that illuminated his soul. Loving the entire humanity, praising others, accepting mistakes promptly, looking at every one with equal eyes etc were the qualities that transformed him not only into a human being but as the greatest man of the century.

Gandhiji along with his ideas has become an ideal for the west also. If we accept gandhian philosophy and his ideals as the ideals of management, we will be able to create our own identity at international level and can make our support more valuable.

Gandhi and Management

Praveen Shukla

Published by
Diamond Pocket Books Pvt. Ltd.
X-30, Okhla Industrial Area, Phase-II
New Delhi-110020
Phone : 011-40712200
E-mail : sales@dpb.in
Website : www.diamondbook.in

Ghandhi and Management
Praveen Shukla

Dedicated to

To the Gandhian thinker and
famous writer
Padma Bhusan Sri Vishnu Prabhakar Ji

Gandhi and His Management

Introduction

It is fascinating to probe that the entire world is finding the methods of social and economic development through the Gandhism which was practised and pioneered by a man called Mahatma Gandhi who was born in a small place named Porbandar in Gujrat. He practised truth and non-violence that are relevant even in this modern world. In fact it has become more relevant in this modern era. Today when a lot of people were killed in terrorist attack then the only man that comes into mind is none other than Mohan Das Karam Chand Gandhi and his philosophy. Gandhiji himself said "My life is my message." Today people who are working in the field of management should try to practise Gandhism to work efficeiently. To accomplish various kinds of works Gandhi ji applied the management that is still providing light to many common people and their life.

Any body wants to become a management guru has to imbibe those qualities. Without these qualities no one can be a successful businessman or a management guru.

For being a successful management guru one has needed to understand the time and the condition, the psychology of colleagues, character building ability, organizational capacity, standard thinking process, sense of duty, honour for time, laborious , positive attitude, organized, inspiring, cracking goals, ability to take decisions, ability to use resources in best possible manner, balanced even in adverse condition and health conscious. While studying Gandhian philosophy it seems that he created his own standards of balancing everything . Citing his success Lari Collins and Daminik Lapier say " In an era when there were no television, radio and such things , people of India were mostly illiterate. Mahatma Gandhi proved that he was a master of mass communication because he had an extra ordinary talent . It is quite sure that when historians and editors will select man and women of the century this man will be topped in the list ."

Gandhiji spearheaded a lot of movements . He galvanized millions of Indians and created a massive power of common men. Those movements shacked the foundations of British Empire. The colonial rulers understood that they were competing with a man whose policies were not easily dissmantable . Gandhiji galvanized millions of Indians not only physically but he prepared them to win self rule.He launched a lot of movements not only at the level of administration but against the castism and economic inequalities in the society .

The ideals constituted by Gandhiji are not only relevant in our social life but these are very much practical in corporate world. People like the CEO of Boston Consulting Group Mr. Arun Mehra, Management Guru CK Prahalad, Professor of Economics Mr. Arindam Choudhary accept that they have to follow Gandhism to expand their business.

Recently on the occasion of Non Residential Indian Day in Delhi Mr. CK Prahalad said, "It is very important to implement Gandhism for the overall development of our society. If we want to accelerate our GDP we need to follow Gandhian Philosophy."

When he returned back from South Africa and applied his own methods of fighting against the British Empire , it was beyond anybody's expectation that such a common man can create power of common people that would be unbeaten. But he proved himself. He was not a management trainee. How did he mould the common men's ideas into his own ideas ? How did he inspired those millions of peoples to follow him ? How did he prove that truth, non-violence and 'Charkha' can be the instruments of social political, and economic transformations? How did he laid that if millions of people of India of different castes and creeds, poor and rich, man and women would launch movement against the mighty Empire, would be unanswerable. What was that element that drived so many people to follow him ? He said, "Spin cotton thread" and people obeyed that. When he said to denounce foreign clothes people burnt all foreign clothes. He moved forward to break Salt Law and every one stood up to break the law. This was definitely the light of his charismatic personality, ideas and way of living that inspired every Indians. There was no difference in his words and deeds. And this is where his mastery over management is proved.

He managed the power of common people's power in such a way that the Bitishers accepted mentally that they had to leave India very soon. This happened because of the management of Mahatma Gandhi. I feel that he mastered all the qualities of management through his learning and experience of life. Every single idea established by him whether his message, dress, lifestyle, way of talking on burning issues of the society reflects that . A management guru is visible in all these aspects because what he targeted he cracked. To accomplish tasks without any hassle is called management.

Gandhiji said that he was neither a philosopher nor a ideologist. He himself said that he did not want to impose any philosophy or idea that would be considered as a liability. It was the experience of life , truth and non-violence through which he solved all sorts of problems.It seems to me that he was a practical ideologist and a true devotee of 'karma'. That is why in comparison to other leaders Gandhiji is nearer to the Indian culture and people's heart. He was a veteran communicator who used all means of communication like speeches, articles and many more. It is very important for any management guru to communicate at its best. Gandhi ji was master of it. He was so influential that everybody would start following whatsoever his ideas might be.

He experimented so many things that had never been practised by any one. This also establishes his management skill because it is important for a successful management guru not only to follow the traditions but to establish new ideas successfully. Gandhiji had firm belief on his ideas and was confident that these experiments could not be unsuccessful ever.

Gandhiji was the leader of a lot of movements in his life. I would like to mention few of the movements like the srike in Ahmedabad, Khilafat Movement, Champaran Movement, Bardoli Satyagrah, Dandi March, Boycott Movement, Movement for the grant of Harijans entry in the temple and the Quit India Movement. The art of management is omnipresent. He used to analyse the situation earlier and formulated tactics accordingly. And then he motivated physically and mentally all those who were the part of those movements. If we consider the example of Champaran Movement we can see that no other leader had ever employed such tactics earlier in India.

The Empire that never saw the sunset in its territory failed to understand Gandhi's management theory and its practical implications. American management guru Peter Drewker said "The focus of manangement is to motivate people and guide them. Management works at the root level of society. For implementing policies, any management manager should understand that the ideology ,traditions, culture of workers and formulate policies accordingly. I am working with a lot of different companies for long years. On the basis of my experience I can say that management is a spiritual quality. There is an angel and a demon within a human being. Through management he should be provided the freedom in such a way that he can use his knowledge, his freedom and his leadership quality to its best."After analyzing Gandhi's life and his working style you will feel that he used all these qualities as the basis of his policies.

According to the management theory a good management guru should possess treasure of knowledge, discipline, transparency, ability to avoid discrimination and the power to analyse situations as well as himself. It is important to note that Gandhiji did not formulated his policies on the basis of these qualities but when we analyse his life style we feel that all these were natural part of him. Gandhi is not a management manager but in modern time anybody can be successful management manager practising Gandhism and can set new standards because all these qualities of management are visible in it. It was because of his virtues that Einstine once said , "Posterity will not believe that there was a man named Mahatma Gandhi in this world."

A lot of literature on Gandhi and his literary creations had been studied extensively. To prove my points I have added relevant examples in this book. For the Hindi version of his biography published by 'Sasta Sahitya Mandal' the original auto-biography *'My experiment with the Truth'* and for *'Adhi raat ko aajadi'* the original name of the book *'Freedom at mid night'* has been cited. I believe that while reading this book you will feel you are studying such a research work on Gandhi's management skill that has been presented in very simple and interesting way by the author.

William James of Howard University says "If you are thinking transformation in your life, then start it at this very moment with enthusiasm." I feel that if we want to be successful in service or industries then there is a need to understand the nuances of Gandhism . I personally have felt a lot of changes in my life after studying him. Once Gandhi himself said, "Small matters test our principles." Let us start to follow Gandhian ideals since today itself. You may start it with reading this book. You may feel that this is a very small matter, but Gandhi ji himself said " Small matters bring sense of completeness in life and this is not a small matter."

–Praveen Shukla
4649/15-A, New Modern Sahadara
New Delhi 110032

Contents

1

Working Area and Knowledge of Culture

There are no such elements in other cultures as in ours. We have not identified that, we have been taught to avoid studying it and to consider these elements as inferiors. We have almost left to practice them in our behavior. Without good conduct, the intellectual knowledge is just like a lifeless body that is kept safe with the help of chemicals. That might look attractive but it can't inspire. My religion orders me that I learn my culture, accept it and follow it.

India of My Dreamsm page 140

Working Area & Knowledge of Culture

It is very important for a businessman to understand at first the actual conditions of the market . Gandhi's life and thoughts throw a lot of light on it. When Gandhi came back to India and took part in Kolkata conferernce of Indian National Congress in 1901, he decided at that moment that before entering into the public life, he would visit all over India. He said that he would travel in third class compartment to understand the needs of common people and would also try to find out the needs, sufferings and the condition of the poor.

He is of the view that before the commencement of any mission whether it is related to business or life, we should analyse the things at their elementary level. We can not find the right direction until we understand its basic nature and needs.

"Success is not related with failure. But the real success is to achieve whatever is the ultimate goal. It means it is important to win the battle not the quarrels."

Dressing Sense

When Gandhiji returned India from South Africa, he abandoned western dresses. He started wearing 'Dhoti-Kurta', a traditional Indian dress because he was aware of the fact that the dress must be according to the people with whom he had to work. It denotes the fact that in public life your personality and dressing sense also reflects your lifestyle and attitude.

Arindam Choudhary says, "The example of Mahatma Gandhi is the best one to express our civilization and culture. Even today we are stuck in finding out what is good or bad? A leader will never ask his supporters to do something that they can't. Because successful management guru wants to utilize the abilities and resources of all those who are associated with it to its maximum level to achieve his goal. And Mahatma Gandhi has tried to use this during all his movements."

Selection of torch-bearer

Gandhiji considered Gopal Krishna Gokhle as his ideal as well as political guru because he saw the glimpse of dedication for Indian culture and his own ideologies in him. Accepting Gopal Krishna Gokhle as his Guru, he compared him with two other great leaders of that time in this way, "I consider Sir Feroz Shah as Himalaya and Lokmanya as a sea. Gokhle seems to be the Ganga. I can dip in that. I can't climb on the Himalaya. There is a fear of drowning in the sea. But one can play in the lap of Ganga and enjoy boating."

Gandhiji followed all the policies of Gokhale during his entire life. Even after Gokhle's demise Gandhi said accepting his power, "In the field of politics, Gokhle had created a special place in my heart during his life and even after his death no one can replace him."

Affirming his confidence in Gokhale, Gandhiji said, "There was no need to try to enter in the society for me during his life time. I just had to follow his orders and his wishes. I liked this condition. Before entering into the Indian cyclone I needed "a touch-bearer" for me and I was safe under his aegis."

Above thoughts reflect that Gandhiji was dedicated towards Gopal Krishna Gokhle during the latter's life and after his death. Because his principles and dedication always remained same. Gandhiji accepted whosoever he did that from bottom of his heart and always tried to follow and adopt their principles and policies. For any successful management guru it is very important to formulate principles and afterwards follow them. Considering Gandhism one should pay attention on following facts:

- Have adequate knowledge of working area.
- Dressing sense and lifestyle must be in congruence with the mentality of the colleagues of the working area.
- Use the ability and resources to the maximum level to achieve the goal.
- Select the guide after giving the second thought.
- Believe in others and maintain their belief.

❑

2

Actual Analysis of The Condition

There is not an iota of suspicion in my mind that in a country like ours, where millions of people are unemployed , it is very important to keep them engaged in certain works so that they may earn their livelihood honestly. There is the need of 'khadi' and 'small scale industries'. For me, it is as clear as sun that these industries are the demand of the day. I do not know what will happen to them in the future and I am not bothered to know it .

–Sampurna Gandhi Vangmay {part 64} page no. 195

Actual analysis of the condition

Neither can you be a successful businessman nor can you take any decision until you do not understand your ability and capacity. These days it is often heard that a student was preparing for civil services and all of a sudden he committed suicide because of the undesired results. All these incidents prove that these students do not analyse their abilities and capacities. They set their aims high but they do not have the quality to achieve that.

Gandhiji considered this very carefully. He analysed his own abilities and capacity properly and accordingly formulated his policies to fight against the British. It was only because of his policies that once the British Viceroy Mike Vevel said angrily, "There is no remedy of this old man. What should we do with him?" There is victory of Gandhji in this line. In order to achieve the goal, he managed his policies in such a way that his opponents had no any answer to that.

The reservoir of experience

Gandhiji's life was like gold which had gone through fires to reach that stage. He spent times in England and South Africa during his studies which extended the horizon of his personality not only at the level of principle but also at the practical level too. In South Africa when Gandhiji was looking for a room in the hotel in Johanesburg , he was not provided any. When he narrated the story to his host Abdulla Seth,he replied, "How can they allow us?"Gandhiji asked, "Why?" Abdulla Seth's answer was, "You will understand this soon. We only can live in this country. If we have to earn money these derogations have be tolerated."

From that very moment, Gandhiji started experiencing that this human discrimination was unethical and inhuman. The condition of Indians was miserable at that time in South

Africa. Describing the plight of Indians, he has said, "We are known as 'Coolie' in South Africa. In our country, coolie means a labour but in South Africa it means a sweeper and other derogatory meanings. The area that has been allotted to live these people are called, coolie location. There was such a location in Johansberg and there were other such locations at different places. And those are still there. There were no ownership rights for Indians.

Discussing the condition of South Africa he has said that the barbers were not permitted to do hair dressing of these coolies. Gandhiji kept himself cool in every condition and kept analyzing the things correctly ,so he thought also on this condition. "In reality, it was not the barber who was responsible for that . His occupation will be ruined if he starts doing hair cut for black-skinned. In fact, we also not let the barbers of upper caste Hindus to offer similar services to the people of lower castes.I have been punished for this many times in South Africa and that was the result of our deeds."

The division on the basis of untouchability , colour discrimination and casteism is a blot on humanism. Following are his thoughts regarding untouchability and discrimination:

- Untouchability is a curse for our country.
- The upper caste Hindus ought to treat the children of harijans as their own.
- The liars and hypocrites are untouchables.
- I do not wish rebirth but if I have to take rebirth then I will prefer to be born as a untouchable so that I may be able to reduce their sufferings.
- Harijans can not be isolated from the village society because thay are the foundation.
- Indians are already untouchables because of their poverty.
- Even if I am reduced into pieces I will not stop my affinity and love for these dalits.

- If God is one and so is the soul, then there can not be any untouchable.
- Sweepers or untouchables are as worthy of respect as the mother who cleanses her child in the childhood.

All these words clearly state that Gandhiji's thoughts were the outcome of his vast experience. It is very important to face those difficulties that we wanted to dismantle being a successful manager. Because there is a huge gap between theory and practical. If you consider the nuances very minutely before the implementation of principle then the results will be more accurate and useful.

Accept the Goodness

It is the responsibility of a successful management guru to not only criticize others for their mistakes but also to appreciate them for their good qualities. Gandhiji analysed different things in different perspectives. He felt that no any caste is totally right or wrong. Everyone has certain qualities along with some vices. There are a lot of incidents that had formed this opinion. During his travel to South Africa, he met several white people who supported him and behaved sympathetically. He has narrated the situation when during travel in train the guard scolded him for boarding in the first class compartment in this way,"There was only one English traveller in the compartment. He chided the guard, "Why are you creating trouble for this gentleman? Can't you see he has the ticket of first class compartment? I have no problem in letting him sit in the compartment." He said so and saw at me and then said, "You sit comfortably". The guard murmered, "If you are willing to sit with a coolie why should I bother for this?"He went away murmuring these words.

When on the call for 'Direct Action" of the proclamation Jinnah there was a series of communal rights in Kolkatta, Gandhiji was busy in trying to maintain peace in other parts of the country. Later when Lord Mountbatten requested him then he went to Kolkatta to restore peace. There a Muslim named Suhraworthy requested him that his presence in Kolkata could make the things better and he apologized for whatever happened. Gandhiji felt a sense of regret in his voice. Discussing his qualities Daminik Lapier and Lari Collins says, "Gandhiji had a great qualities that he could understand the qualities of his opponents and he used to promote those qualities. He felt that there was a true compassion for the Muslim fellows in the heart of Suhraworthy."

Gandhiji believed that we should listen our opponents carefully before drawing any conclusion against them. We can not understand his motives until we understand his principles and thoughts. He said, "If we understand the thoughts of our enemy, the two-third part of world's grief and doubt will be vanished."

Analysis of Education

Gandhiji had always analysed his time and conditions very accurately as a successful management guru. He was aware of the fact that there would not be any development in the poverty ridden country without the spread of education.That is why, for the development of the country,he always emphasized those points through which a lot of elementary problems could be solved. And because of this he advocated for education vigorously. But he also laid emphasis on the quality education. He said, "It is an offence to pay for a kind of education that is not beneficial either for the country or for the individual. In my opinion, there is no personal gain which cannot be transformed into national benefit. Most of my critics also do accept that the present system of higher education –why only higher education but also the primary and secondary education, has nothing to do anything with reality. And if it is so there is no use of this education for the nation at all."

We fight for our rights but there will not be any real progress as long as the education will be neglected.

Need for Solid Education System

Gandhiji aways preferred practical matters to his principles. He believed that the purpose of education should not be limited just to provide jobs for our youngsters. It should be fashioned to the overall development of our children. He said,"People go to common schools and colleges keeping the job factor in the mind, prepare for examinations and just after coming out of the examination hall they forget all that they have learnt. Most of the people are concerned more about the degree, not about the learnings."

That is why, a successful manangement guru should not be a bookworm but along with that he must be capable of using all these learnings.

Capability of Self-introspection

It is very important for a person associated with the management field to have a quality to introspect. If we are not aware of our abilities then we cannot decide things properly. In such a situation we are dangerous for ourselves as well as the organization we work with. So we should decide the direction of all work as per our capacities and abilities. At first, Gandhiji analysed his own abilities as well as that of the common people and then he decided to move forward with the movements based on truth and non-violence. When he sensed that there might be violence he rolled back the movement. Because he did not want to provide Britishers any such opportunity that could hinder the process of attaining freedom.

It is an excellent example in itself how Gandhiji inspired the whole nation for political, social and economic changes. When we are talking about the Gandhian policies we need to keep one thing in mind that all this happened before independence. There is a huge difference between today and that time. We can not imagine things keeping in mind today's conditions. For the actual knowledge of that era we need to understand the social, economic and political conditions of pre-Independence era.

True Analysis of Village Conditions

Before independence, there was a time when the entire political and economic structure of the nation was dependent on the villages. The Panchayat elections were the elementary level of political institutions. A large portion of revenues were collected from the village farming, irrigation and small industries based in these villages. It was the village society where people knew one another and took part in every body's happiness and sorrow. That is why, Gandhiji initiated all his policies and movements with the association of the common people of villages. He emphasized upon the development of the villages for the overall progress of the country and formulated all his policies for the movements as per the soul of villages. He said, "If villages get destructed India will be ruined. The development of villages is possible only in the condition of their zero exploitation. If the bigger industries will be settled they will definitely exploit the villages community because there will be a huge competitive gap that will hamper the village prospect. So what should be focused is that the villages must be self-dependent and produce things for their own use. If this policy of rural industry will be accepted there is no harm in using modern machineries. Only this should be guaranteed that there will not be any exploitation because of it."

Gandhiji has given much importance to villages in his economic model. He said that we should establish those industries that could develop the creative abilities of the people of villages. Without hampering the natural resources, we should develop our resources and industries. We should establish industries in the small townships in the nearby areas of the village so that people could return to their home.

These industries would be beneficial for the small townships as well as for the villages. He said in this way capital would be accumulated and this would promote green revolution. Gandhiji emphasized to develop the telecommunication at the local level.

Gandhiji never opposed science, machinery and technologies. But he accepted them with few of its shortcomings. In 1924, when a man asked him "Why are you against the modernization?" He replied, "How can I oppose mechanization? I know that our body is assembled of so many machines. Spinning wheel is also a machine. The small 'tooth pick'is also a form of machine. My opposition is not against the machines but to those conditions in which a person gains at the cost of millions of people."

It is a historical fact that before the arrival of East India Company, these villagers were not unemployed but today anyone can see that most of them are unemployed. So there is no need of fresh researches and investigations to understand that if they will not work for six months they will die hungry.

Economic Equality

The meaning of economic equality is to abolish all types of differences between the capitalist and the workers forever. If the rich do not come forward to bridge these differences and allow the share of wealth to flow up to the lowest statra of the society the violence and bloody revolutions is inevitable.

Opposition of Hypocrisy

It is important for a successful management guru to connect himself with the modern technologies and oppose those old traditions that have just become hypocrisy. Gandhiji had firm faith in God but he always opposed those customs that incite hypocrisy. Following incident tells us about his view, "When I grew older many others forced me to wear *'Janau'* in India and also in South Africa but I was not influenced by their arguments. If an untouchable could not wear this why others? I did not find any logic to accept a thing that was not the part of our culture. There was no scarcity of this sacred thread but the logic. I wore *'Kanthi'* because of being a 'Vetetarian'. 'Tuft' or a top knot was forced by the elders. I shaved off my 'tuft' in a fear that there would be the fashion of bare head in the overseas and the white would laugh at me. My nephew Chhagan Lal Gandhi ,who was living with me in south Africa, had 'Tuft'. I considered that as a hindrance in his pubic work and because of this fear I had his tuft shaved off. In this way, I was ashamed of 'tuft'."

He did not only oppose the hypocrisy but also contributed extensively for the women education and their overall development in the society. Gandhiji was aware of the fact that for making India a superpower it was important to elevate women's condition. He said, "As long as the social taboos like child marriage, considering marriage the most important affair for girls, marriage before puberty, ban on widow marriage etc will remain, the plight of women can't end."

Synchronisation with Common People

There will be no other ideal than Mahatma Gandhi if you are a kind of person who needs support from various people to accomplish your task. As a successful management guru, Gandhiji always formulated his policies as per the beat of time. He had become the heart beat of all those who were working with him. Commenting on this aspect of Gandhiji Larry Collins and Dominique Leperre says " Gandhiji was so much associated with the life of common people, their grief and joys that he had garnered an extraordinary quality of sensing the mood of the country. His followers used to say that he was like a veteran of ancient Indian stories who suddenly trembled while he was experiencing fire in front of a hearth. He said to one of his disciples, "Look outside, there is a poor man trembling in the cold. When the disciple saw outside he was surprised to see a man was standing there. The disciples of Gandhiji said that he was able to understand the soul of India easily in this similar way."

For synchronization with others, Gandhiji has emphasized upon following facts:

- To understand one's real nature one should adjudge itself neutrally.
- We can not see our vice as we can not see our back.
- When somebody breaks one law the process of unlimited breaking starts.
- We are only responsible for our conditions.
- There will be definite manipulations if there is an element of selfishness in the act.
- Nectar transforms into poison if even a drop of poison get mixed with it.

Actual Understanding of Time

Those who wait can get only those things that are left behind by fighters.

For me, it is not very important what have you achieved, but more important is that when you achieve? For mastering this ability one has to develop a sense to understand the beat of time. Few people say how is it possible that the way Gandhiji has described the concept of 'satyagrah' and non-violence forced the Britishers to leave India? To the contrary,

Gandhiji created power by uniting the society as per his policies and then he raised the voice against imperial power which no critic has mentioned. This is mentioned in the *'Freedom At Midnight'*- "At the mid night of 8th August 1942 in a conference room in Bombay where heat was creating suffocations, Gandhiji gave a call to all his followers of All India Congress Committee to fight. His voice was calm and composed but it was surprising to hear such excited and emotional words from Gandhiji's mouth."

When Gandhiji felt that now we had to talk directly with Britishers. Then he felt that Indian freedom struggle had reached at a stage where direct talk with the imperial power could be done, then he said, "I want freedom immediately." He also said, "If it is possible let it be in the night before the dawn."

"I am giving you a very small mantra" , he said his followers "that mantra is *'Do or Die'*. Whether we will win freedom or die in a bid to achieve it. We will not be alive to witness the perpetuality of this slavery."

It is very important for a successful management guru to ascertain the actual condition and use the accumulated power at an opportune time for the perfect execution of the plans. His decisions taken at that times are still relevant in this modern era and provide us new energy and warmth to move forward.

Let us implement these qualities of Gandhiji's working style in our life:

- The actual analysis of the conditions is very important before working in any area.
- Accumulate experience and make the knowledge practical accordingly.
- Accept other's qualities and implement them in our life. We ought to behave in such a way that we expect to be behaved.

- Believe on others and help them in the moment of crisis.
- Accepting the value of education and vow to enrich our knowledge continuously.
- Practice equality and oppose hypocrisy.
- Create a synchronized friendly environment with your colleagues.
- Ascertain your motive and the path to achieve it as per time, condition and the atmosphere.

❑

3

Character Building Ability

I believe and have experienced many a time that even if someone is very talented, his secretly done misdeeds affect his work. There is a firm basis of this rule and that is the person who works needs a policy. Those are successful who have a blameless character even though there is lack of suitability in them.

\- *Sampurna Gandhi Wangmay(Section-64) Page No-175*

Character Building Ability

It is mandatory to establish an ideal for the leader who leads any movement, an institution or a business. If you are not able to influence your colleagues they will not accept your leadership. For this, you will have to mould your character in such a way that it will be visible to all. It was the ability of Gandhiji that he followed his ideals from the bottom of his heart which provided power to his character that made him popular at national and international levels.

Gandhiji's unique quality was that he accepted the working ability and ideas on different issues of his opponents also. Gandhiji always strived to abolish all sorts of social problems no matter what would be the cost. At the time of partition when communal riots broke out in the country, he said that I was willing to die if it could extinguish the fire of communal riot.

According to Mahatma Gandhi, there are seven kinds of heinous sins- Wealth without labour, Pleasure without soul, Knowledge without character, Business without morality, humanity without science, Sacrifice without religion and Politics without principles.

Regarding the character building he has said :

- Good behavior is the ladder of character.
- Character is the most precious thing of life.
- Knowledge without character becomes an evil power, which has been exemplified by lots of cunning thieves and well behaved criminals across the world.
- The character of nation can be ascertained considering its people's character.
- The process of character building is not a trivial affair. We cannot develop without it even after getting freedom.
- Character is the most important wealth in the world.

- Character must be protected at any cost.
- There is no any important work as character building for the educated.
- The motive of education should be character building. The real education is one which develops courage, multiplies qualities and enhances the hunger of achieving higher goals consistently.
- If we build character of individuals, the society will be able to take care of it. People developed in such a way should be the leaders of the society.
- Self-confidence is the first condition of character building process.
- If there is no character building then all the creativity will be ruined.

Development of Human Qualities

In absence of human quality none can be a successful management guru. We need to develop human qualities in ourselves in such a way that no one remain unaffected of it whosoever comes in the contact. A man cannot be socially recognized if he does not have a character irrespective of his wealth. Your success depends on the fact that your qualities must be acknowledged by the society. If there are no human qualities in a human being, he is a satan in the guise of a human being. To the contrary if a satan possesses certain qualities like humbleness, love for youngesters, respect for elders, dedication towards colleagues, dedication towards work and the importance of labour etc then a human being is there inside him. On this subject, Gandhiji has said,"A human being will be able to see his true character only when he understands very clearly that it is mandatory to throw the inhuman qualities out of himself. Even though we are human anatomically, still we are as our earliest forefathers in the absence of non-violance in the life."

A true management guru is one who can opt right path for himself and can guide others as well in a right direction. If a man himself is not on the right path, he cannot guide others . Gandhiji says on this topic, "Can a matchbox light other woods if it has not spark in it? How a man himself misdirected can be guide of others? Those who are drowned himself, how can they save others?"

Man is a social animal. He has first obligations towards the family in which he took birth. His second obligation is towards the society of which his family is a part. And the third one is towards his country which provides everything to live. Someone who has started the process of the development of the family, the process of his contribution in the development of society and the country starts at that very moment. It is the responsibility of a true manager that he himself acts in such a way that should be helpful in the development of the family,society and country and inspire others to follow him. Let us discuss some of the virtues that enable a common man to become a successful management guru.

Importance of Love

I believe that to love it is important to be loved. Here it is also important to understand the broad meaning of 'love'. Instead of loving any particular human being if you start loving the entire nature there will be a definite transformation in your horizon of thought. This is an important ingredient of a human character building. One who hates instead of love cannot be a great human being. That is why Gandhiji has said on this subject, "One whose heart is filled with love can not harm others. Love can only be expressed through self-abhorance and self-purification."

Love is the most powerful in the world and at the same time most humble. Love suffers but never expresses any anger or seek revenge. It is only through power of love that has elevated a lot of great people like Jesus, Socraty and

Gandhi to the status of God. There is no place of fear where love resides. There is nothing impossible for a pure form of love in the world. This is only the love that has saved the life on the earth so far. There had been numerous a time blood-shedding on the earth that might have lost its existence if there had not been love. In my opinion, there will not be any character building of a management guru if there is not the element of love in his life. He will not be able to influence anybody. Describing the greatness of love Gandhiji says, " The life survives in between the destructions. That is why there must be a bigger force than this. There only may be an organized kind of society that is a worth living. If this is the rule of life then this must be implemented in the daily life. In a situation where conflict arises, the resolution should be derived from love. I have implemented this very simply in my life."

Gandhiji's Opinion Regarding Love

- If love resides in the heart, nothing should be decided through means of violence.
- My imagination of love is that it is softer than flowers and harder than rocks.
- Love remains happy with truth, tolerates everything, accepts everything and be hopeful along with the fact that it never goes in vain.
- God resides where there is love.
- We should extend the limit of love from home to village, village to district, district to state and state to the entire nation and across the globe.

Morality

A successful management guru is an ideal for his follower. People follow his style of performing things. That is why he should constitute such an ideal through his activities that will follow the path of morality. Gandhiji's acts in this direction are exceptional. He always emphasized the need to establish morality. He believed that any improvement whether it may be political, social, economic or any other field must be associated with the morality. He says, "It is not only important that the moral excercises be done through pure means but also that it must not be under any pressure. If I rise early in the morning only out of fear of losing the job is not morality. Similarly I live in austerity and simplicity does not reflect any moral play. But if I am a rich person and still I live in austerity and simplicity only because of the poverty spread around me constitutes morality."

There is a famous maxim in India, 'Do good and cast it into the river'. We believe in fair play. We should not live morality behind even if there are critics of those acts .

Gandhiji has also accepted this truth, " There must not be an iota of arrogance about our fair works nor should be rated in any kind. However, there must be a constant desire to be better and serve others more than earlier. The works done in the pursuance of such desires are called morality."

Politeness

Dedication and politeness are very important for being successful in the eyes of Gandhiji. He never hated his opponents. He was of the opinion that anybody who rose in his life should become more humble than earlier. Because arrogance ruins the man's mind. That is why he said, "we should follow the example of mango tree whose branches draw lower as it bears fruits. This politeness is its jewel."

Gandhiji believed that his theory of non-violence and truth led people towards politeness. So he said, " The feeling of non-violence leads towards politeness. Non-violence means to have full faith in God who is always there to protect everybody. If we want to support Him , we should abandon arrogance and offer our prayer with repenting heart."

Remember this, politeness is rewarded with politeness. Practice it as much as possible. Initially it will demand some efforts but it proves very precious. Politeness is the trademark of a good human being. Politeness is the part of courtesy which benefits the whole organization.

The Value of Commitment

It is well said, "Degraded people talk about others, common people talk about things and great people talk about advice."

Character provides commitment which boosts confidence. Here the meaning of commitment is that our acts must be in congruence of our words. There must not be any difference.

"We should take oath to behave lovingly with younger, kindly with elders, compassionately with strugglers and weak, in tolerance with falters because we must pass through any of these states even once during our life span."

Respect for Mother Tongue

Gandhiji did not abandon using his mother tongue Gujrati even when he was active in South Africa. He believed that even though we leant a lot of languages in the pursuance of knowledge but we had to save our family traditions and to make our children moral then we should use our mother tongue. Citing the example of his conversation with Pollok, Gandhiji said, "There has been a hot discussion between me and Pollok regarding the education of these children. I have believed right from the beginning that those parents who force their children to speak in English even in home are actually anti-nationalists. I also believed that these children remain deprived of the cultural and social heritage of the country. And at the end of the day they become less willing to serve the nation and people. Because of this belief I always speak in Gujarati with the children."

Dedication Towards Education

Once a man came to famous French Philosopher and said, " I would have been a good human being if I could have mind like you. Pascal replied, " Be a good human being , your mind will become like me".

- Our mind needs good ideas just like food for our body.
- Good education promotes good thinking.
- If you do something for others , do that with utmost honesty for the sake of God.

None can progress in their life without accepting the value of education. It is very important for a successful manager to enhance his knowledge constantly. He must be up-to-date with all sorts of experiments in the history as well as in the present time. And only education can help in it.

Gandhiji always emphasized the role of education but his focus was on practical education. He said, "I want to amend the college education in such a way that it suits national interest. I am not an enemy of higher education but I am against the kind of education imparted in the country. I have seen that this higher education has misled a lot many pursuers of higher education; but this does not mean that there should not be higher education. I will say higher education to these which makes a man more polite, kind and dedicated."

The Power of Soul

There was a man who earned his bread out of selling balloons in the fares. He had red, yellow, blue and green colored balloons. He used to set free a balloon filled with Helium gas in the air whenever his income lowered. Looking at that flying balloon children wished to have a balloon like that. They bought balloons and his selling grew up. This was his daily routine. Once he was selling balloons in a market. Suddenly he felt that someone was pulling his shirt. When he turned back he saw there was a child. That child asked that balloon-seller, "If you set free this black balloon ,will it fly?". Those words of that child touched his heart and he replied, " Son ! the balloon does not fly because of its color but what is being filled in it."

Develop Good Habits

A man with good habits is considered to be a man of character and the vice-versa. Habits are more powerful than arguments and understanding. "Make good habits because habits build the character."

It is hard to adopt good habits but it makes life easier. And it is easy to practice bad habits but it makes life harder. That is why we need two kinds of knowledge. One that enables us to earn bread and other that teaches us the way of living. Gandhiji took both types of education simultaneously. He was conscious about the fact that there must not be any germination of bad habits within him since childhood. He did introspection from time to time and was in constant touch with the great literary creations and inspirational incidents of life.

Harishchandra's Play

It is an incident of Gandhiji's childhood. A drama company came to his village and he got the permission to see that. It was the story of Harishchandra. He was not satisfied to see that drama once and was eager to see that more, but there was no permission for it. He repeatedly remembered that play for long time in his mind. He kept thinking why are people not like Harishchandra? He thought that suffering like Harishchandra and sticking with truthfulness was life. He believed that the sufferings of the Harishchandra in the play were true. He used to weep in the remembrance of those sufferings of Harishchandra. He firmly believed that all should follow the path of truth. The characters of Harishchandra and Sharavan Kumar will always remain alive in his conscience through the childhood plays and literature.

Emphasis on Discipline

The key of management is discipline. None can achieve success without being disciplined. For being a successful man, one has to extend his working area slowly. It is not so important just to extend the limits of work but to accomplish them properly. If we have only extended work field and have not organized it properly, everything will be disorganized. And only discipline can reorganize it. There is rarely any other example of disciplined life as Gandhiji's. It was his discipline and organizational abilities that enabled him to accomplish a lot of tasks simultaneously. Gandhiji believed that there were two parts of discipline; one is physical and other is mental discipline which is important for management abilities. Following are the ideas of Gandhiji about discipline :

- The training of discipline should be initiated since childhood at the home itself.
- No any institution can run efficiently in absence of discipline. Actually discipline is the key of unity and the ladder of development.
- Discipline is not only meant for defence personnel but also for everybody to maintain in various spheres of life.
- It is possible to maintain discipline only when you are very much interested in doing your work. Without it, discipline will only be imitable.
- The discipline of the citizens of any country reveals the introduction of the nation.
- Inner discipline must be maintained in the same way as the discipline in outer world.
- Self-discipline is the mother of all disciplines. Do not expect disciplined behavior until you yourself do not follow that.

We do not have any right to impose discipline on others until we ourselves do not follow it. That is why, I feel that for being a successful manager it is important to be inspired by Gandhiji. We should start maintaining discipline at the earliest.

Hunger for Knowledge

Gandhiji believed, "There is no limit of knowledge". Even after 60 years of his death the entire world remembers him and draws inspiration from this great Indian. What was unique in that man? Everybody has its answer. He had his most precious thing i.e. 'experience-born knowledge'. He had an instinct to find out new facts and to understand different behaviors . Once one of his followers asked him, " Bapu ! At times you decline your own words. You say differently at different times in the same matter?" Gandhiji replied, "I try to learn new things everyday and when you constantly extend your horizon of knowledge , you start disbelieving your own perceptions after a certain period of time." He also said had I expressed different views at different times then latter one was my ultimate thought. This is similarly very important for a successful management guru to enhance his horizon of knowledge permanently and be aware of all new experiments taking place in the universe.

These are certain beliefs of Gandhiji about Knowledge:

- There will not be freedom in true sense without proper knowledge.
- Knowledge is the light without which we can not march forward.
- It will be useless if arrogance is associated with knowledge.
- Knowledge ought to be an instrument of character building.
- True knowledge is one which has the potential to reduce human sufferings.

- The knowledge which remains in the brain and does not travel in to the heart proved unfruitful in the experience of life.

Gandiji focused on self-study to enhance knowledge. Self-study means to study yourself and learn new things. This is the best means of gaining knowledge. A man can learn a lot with the help of self study even though he remains at his home. That is why we should stick with self study to become successful in the life . In this regard following are the beliefs of Mahatma Gandhi:

- There is no momentum in the thoughts in the absence of self study.
- There is no any habit as good as self study for the gentleman.
- Self study is the foundation of thinking process.
- Self study is the best habit of learned.
- Mental development is not possible in absence of self study.
- Self study is the best means to accumulate knowledge and self-development.
- Self study is the key to knowledge.

There are a lot of examples of many great people who achieved success on the basis of self study. School or college going students are concerned only about their degrees and certificates. But they start self study when their horizon of knowledge extends and thereafter starts real development. It is very important for a successful management guru to be in touch with self study for ever.

Develop Self-dependence

Self dependence means do your work yourself. In this chapter talked about those talent which cannot be developed without self-dependence. We will have to develop a habit to do own work ourself to motivate others and citing himself as ideal. Self-dependence is the first ladder of success. For a successful management guru, it is important to develop character of self dependence. Gandhiji has said about self dependency in the following words:

- Most of the world's great men were self dependent.
- My only duty is to show the people how can they solve their problems.
- Self dependence is equally important for the individual as well as the society and the nation.
- Self dependence bears the fruit of happiness.
- Every child of the nation should be taught the lesson of self dependence. We should learn it from our western counterparts.

Apply all the learnings of this chapter in the life right from today and make them the part of your lifestyle:

- No any management professional can influence others without building a character.
- We should consistently develop human virtues .
- You can win any heart with the help of love, morality and politeness.
- It is mandatory for ideal character to possess 'commitment'.
- Develop good habits consistently and practice them.
- None can get success in the absence of discipline.
- Hunger for knowledge not only improves knowledge but also enhances confidence.
- Develop the habit of doing own work .

❑

4

Establishment of Self Power

"A country like India, where not only human beings but also the stones are worshipped as God in its farm background, saw a magical power or mahatma in him and wherever he went the entire nation followed him. Undoubtedly, he was the most charismatic person of the century who had powerful magnetic power. He was mahatma for his followers.

–Freedom at Midnight P 36

Establishment of Self Power

Whenever big changes occurred, great revolutions took place, extensive social transformation happened, that had always happened with the support of the people of that country. In 1850, when Karl Marx in his book *"Das Capital"* propounded the new social revolution then many of the workers working in industries always stood with him in his support. A management guru must possess the power in his voice that he can divert others' opinion in his favor. Gandhiji possessed this power in great deal. If management guru has not this power to influence others then he cannot get success. A management guru should develop following qualities to establish self power:

- Establishment of self effect
- Getting public support
- Power to extend thoughts

Based on the above three points, Gandhiji had established the standard of success which makes him the most impressive personality of that era. He did not allow his age to affect his thoughts. Gandhiji did more experiments along with growing time, experience and knowledge. A consciousness developed in him provided him new lease of energy consistently.

Establishment of Self Effect

There is no other example like Gandhiji who has established his thoughts in the heart of millions of Indians. He penetrated the Indian people's mind. He had realized the feeling of Indians very minutely. He prepared plans in accordance with the common people in such a manner that no one was able to overshadow him. His strong rivals could not stay in opposition to him for a longer period of time. Actually he went into the roots of problems and formulated solid plans to root them out. When Gandhiji reached to

South Africa and saw the plight of Indians then he decided that whether he should went back or should protest against color discrimination. Considering the plight of Indians Gandhiji told, "Either I should fight for my rights or should go back, otherwise tolerate the insult. And going Pritoria will be an act of cowardice. The troubles I got is external. It is a symptom of severe disease. This severe disease is color discrimination."

Within a very short span of time, Gandhiji united Indian society in South Africa and convinced them as per his opinion that a revolution must be initiated. Gandhiji who himself was in dilemma whether he would be able to stay or not , felt that a whole class had come , stood by him and were offering their support. It was the power of the management guru in Gandhiji, who in very short span of time and with very limited technology united the whole society. The biggest contributor in his success was discipline. As Gandhiji maintained discipline in his life, it motivated others even without any word. He said, " Those people who cannot control themselves, actually can't control others."

British government had also become the fan of Gandhiji along with Indians. After the freedom, Lord Mountbatten himself requested him to go to Calcutta to bring peace there. Because if the communal riots broke out then it would enfold entire country in to its grip and it would be very tough to control that. It was the establishment of faith among Indian people itself. When Gandhiji reached Noakhali at the age of seventy seven years, his supporters said that it was not safe to go there at this moment. There might be risk at your life. But there was such a fearless man within Gandhiji who could not be deviated from his goal by anybody. At that time, his health started deteriorating, but this had nothing to do with his resolve. Commenting on this journey of Gandhiji, Dominique Lepierre and Larry Collins have written in *'Freedom At Midnight'*, "He had his artificial teeth which he used for eating. Ageing had an impact on his body but he was marching forward even with more determination on the path of duty. He had steel-framed spectacle for his eyes but was able to see the entire world through that. His eyes might loose their sight gradually but he could see the world through his inner eyes which was getting sharper day by day. That's why Britishers were afraid to make eye contact with him."

It was the magic of the policies of Mahatma Gandhi that created such a strong movement not only at political level but also at the social level that was beyond the imagination of the imperial rulers. The freedom struggle of India was a subject of curiosity for the world. The West was surprised to think how could a man galvanized the entire country with the concept of truth and non-violence? How could he transform his ideas as the ideas of the nation? Narrating the way Gandhiji disciplined his freedom fighting followers, Dominique Leperrie and Larry Collins have said, "He did not provide his fighters shiny and medal loaded dresses but simple cotton dress , still those were recognizable from a distance and was feeling a sense of unity among them. This proved equally fruitful as the European dictators' black or maroon shirts."

Gandhiji is a management Guru who inspired people in various spheres of life. He inspires us to mould our thought in such a way that can achieve mass appeal and also get approval of the man regarding whom it has been formulated. Then using this influence we should try to achieve our target.

Mass Appeal

Gandhiji fought to dismantle various traditions and establish them in new format. He was well aware of the fact that in that condition it was not easy for anyone to fight against the imperial power by only means of individual force. That's why he galvanized the entire nation and changed the scenario completely. He knew that there were no other power except the power of common man. And accordingly he used social power to achieve political goals. Ghandhiji believed that if women and children along with men became the part of the national movement then it would be unstoppable. That's why he used his managerial skills to unite all sections of the country.

He felt that it was impossible for any leader in India to unite entire society until he enjoyed mass acceptance. At that time, the social power of the country was divided. This was divided in form of caste, language and different cultures. At first, Gandhiji strived tounite them and was successful in it. People loved his way of communication.

To transform self ideas into the ideas of mass ideas in one of the qualities of a successful management guru. Gandhiji nursed this virtue because he had an understanding of common man ideas. Regarding this quality of Gandhiji it is said, "His communication tools were of ancient times. He used to write all his letters in his own hand, conversed with followers directly during the prayer meetings or Congress meetings. He did not employ any such technique that could promote verbose. He used simple means of communications which touched the heart of millions and that is why his messages reached every nook and corner of the country at a time when there were no modern equipments of communication. It is very surprising to note that he used the technique of fasting successfully in a country which was continuously facing famines and the curse of hunger. This man who drank the water of the Ganga and Yamuna defeated the cola drinkers, English men.

At the time of partition when entire country was in the grip of communal violence, he observed fast against it. His health consultant Dr. Sushila Nayar briefed his health condition daily. When people heard that his condition is deteriorating day-by-day, there was sudden change in the atmosphere. A lot of journalists across the world assembled at Birla House to get the information regarding his health.

All India Radio started a half an hour bulletin daily on Gandhiji's health from the Albukark Road. People assembled in fields with flags in hands across the country and shouted slogans; " Hindu-Muslim Bhai-Bhai", "Hindu-Muslim Be Unite", "Save Gandhiji's Life".

Committees were set up to save Gandhiji's life in which there were people of all the religions across the nation. There was not a single mosque in the country where Muslim did not pray for the life of their beloved leader. "Your life is ours" was a heart touching telegram sent by the untouchables of Mumbai.

This was nothing but Gandhiji's mass acceptance. The fast of a man changes the atmosphere of the nation, shows the level of his mass acceptance. He had developed a unique quality to influence rags to riches of the nation. Dominique Leperrie and Leri Collins describe this ability in the following words, "Gandhiji created a breeze that had to transform into a cyclone. And accordingly surprising changes were inevitable at Delhi which was not very enthusiastic about his fasts initially. People were coming out of streets, markets, villages shouting slogans like waves of cyclone. All shops were closed in honour of Mahatma Gandhi. Schools and colleges were shut. 200 widows and refugees in Punjab refused to accept ration and observed fast on that day to express their love for him."

This must be a part of a successful manager to convince people as per his ideas. Everybody who comes in contact must be in consonance with him mentally.

Surprised Viceroy

When Gandhiji started observing fast against the communal riots , Lord Mountbatton came to see him along with his wife. Gandhiji's health was deteriorating every moment. The Ex-Viceroy was amazed to see that there was a glimpse of naughtiness on Gandhiji's face even thogh he was going through such a phase of physical suffering. He was smiling all the time.

He welcomed the Lord and his wife Advina and said, "Ok! I have to observe fast ,then the mountain comes to Muhammad".

Gandhiji's condition was very critical. His voice had been lowest. Advina Mountbatton was very sad to see this. She came out of Gandhiji's room and started crying. Her husband consoling her said, "Why are you upset ! He is doing what he wants to do. In fact, this little man is very powerful".

This was the power of Gandhiji's principles and personality that left impressions on the Ex-Viceroy. It is very important for a management guru to fashion his policies in a such a manner that it must be acknowledged by the society.

Ability of Expanding the Ideas

There was another strong power in Gandhiji that he transformed his ideas into the ideas of the society. He propounded his thoughts in the society in such a way that it became the central thought of the society. And this is the example of his excellent managerial abilities.

He has shown this ability many a time during numerous movements. Let's see the example of Dandi March.It would have been futile if he would have gone there and had broken the rule. During the march, he popularized his ideas in such a way that entire nation backed him. This incident clearly establishes the fact that he was the master of Indian psychology and was a great communicator. It reflects his true managerial skills.

Gandhism has become very popular in the West also. If we follow the footprints of his managerial skills, it is possible to create a better space for ourselves at the international level even today.

According to Gandhiji, if you want to achieve the 'Truth', you need to follow the path of non-violence. Before launching any movement, Gandhiji used to collect data related to it, analyzed them according to Indian psychology and then formulated policies based on the principle of truth and justice. He planned things in such a way that the enemy was helpless. They did not know how to counter Gandhiji because the whole society was with him. He created such circumstances for the enemy where they could oppose Gandhiji because that would be a moral degradation along with social. He was aware of the fact that a fight against the imperial rulers was possible only with non-violence as a weapon because the rulers had all means of violence to crush any violent uprising. He won the confidence of common people and the media and then in a gradual process he forced the British to surrender. Along with this he also convinced everybody that his fight was for the betterment of the society on the whole. He applied self-restraint for this even at times when he himself was facing crisis. This self-restraint developed as his strength. Everybody started feeling that Gandhiji's voice was their voice. He was a kind of person who was preserver of society with the means of eradicating all sorts of social evils and establishing an ideal society. The poor loved him because they felt that he was their *messiah*. The rich loved him because they thought that following the Gandhiji's ideals they could use their wealth in the best possible manner.

The non-violent spinning wheel to counter the imperial rule became his most promising tool. He associated not only the males but millions of females with the freedom struggle. At that time it was not feasible for females to come out on the roads to protest but with the idea of spinning wheel, female realized that they could contribute a lot even though they remain in the four walls. They considered that their contribution through the spinning wheel might support the Indian freedom struggle and this happened as well. Spinning wheel became the symbol of freedom struggle. It was beyond the belief of the imperial rulers that such a small machine can bring so much trouble for them. Gandhiji used his managerial skills to shake economic foundation of the British rule. Comparing the personalities of Mahatma Gandhi and Lord Mountbatten at the time when they first met, Dominique Leperrie and Larry Collins said, "Fair complexioned, handsome Mountbattan had a physically fit body whereas Gandhiji was very thin and lean. One a worshipper of non-violence and other a brave soldier; one a rich person other who had vowed to live the life of the poorest man on the earth; one was Mountbatten, who used the equipments of communication in the best possible manner during the war and was always looking for new developments in it and was a great General whereas Mahatma Gandhi was the messiah of farmers who remained away from all kinds of paraphernalia , still created such a bond with the common people that none had reached to that in the world."

In the 20th century,1 Gandhiji was the only leader, who not only illuminated the entire world but also created place in the heart of millions. Mahatma Gandhi was not a man but an ideology; a kind of ideology that provided light to the entire humanity and went away. He may go into oblivion as the sun covered with clouds but can not set for ever.

When Europe was full of roaring dictators, at that time Gandhiji spoke gently and revolutionized the most populous state in the world. He never galvanized his followers in the name of power and resources but interestingly he warned them, "If you want to follow me, then there may be chances to fire your own houses to meet the requirements. So, come with me only those who are prepared to sleep without beds, wear khadi, eat simple meal and even ready to clean the night soil of their own."

He attracted the world attention towards Indian freedom struggle on the basis of his ideas. He said, "The entire world is looking at us curiously because we have adopted new methodologies for the freedom struggle which are unique. World has become exhausted of bloody wars. It is looking for a new way to get out of it and I am congratulating myself with a confidence that may the ancient land of India be credited with new path of liberation."

It was his personality that filled tears in the eyes of Mountbattan at the time of former's demise. Mountbattan was very impressed with this simple living saint of Indian soil. Paying his tribute to Gandhiji after the latter's death Mountbattion said, " Gandhiji is as great as Buddha and Jesus in the history of mankind."

A successful management guru should develop such skills that even if his opponent gets acquainted with his skills may not remain aloof from it. Gandhiji had developed an art to formulate principles on the basis of his ideas, life-style, along with the understanding of common man, which transformed him into the greatest leader of that era. Adopt following ideas of Gandhiji's life in your life:

- Develop your personality in such a way that others may derive inspiration out of it.
- Apply your ideas in such a way that it may win your colleagues' acceptance.
- Establish your ideas emphatically so that the positive impression may reflect on others.

❑

5

Awareness About Duty

There is no need to bother about results once the duty is performed. Duty has to be performed whether there is anybody to help or not.

–Sampurn Gandhi Wangmay[Part 67] Page No. 151

Awareness about Duty

Knowing the rights and duties is the important part of the management theory. Gandhiji always understood the ethics of management very minutely. He emphasized that we should perform our duties in complete awareness. He said that if we were not aware of our duties there is no right to ask the rights.

Dedication Towards Principles

Gandhiji believed that none could perform their duties in the state of ignorance of principles. He felt that principles must be followed at any cost. He has said in this context, "There are some perpetual principles that can not be compromised. Even death should be embraced for these principles; after all principles are principles. We should strive continuously to follow these principles and these efforts ought to be wise, aware and firm."

Gandhiji had set many examples during his life that establishes that the principles of duties ought to be followed in the practical life. He believed that there was no right to demand any right if we did not follow the path of duty. He said, "The right to perform duties is most important in one's life. All the judicial rights of human being are inherent in it." A successful management guru should vow to perform duties at any cost.

Incidents that Reflect the Sense of Duty

Setting many examples Gandhiji had shown that performance of duty should be utmost priority. What was the quality with which Gandhiji galvanized a society that was divided in the name of caste, creed and religion? That had been the dedication to perform duties. He never altered his path. He accepted all his mistakes publically and also begged pardon. It is very important for a successful management guru to perform his duties with full dedication and always be ready to accept and rectify the mistakes whenever found any.

Himself Worked as a Midwife

When his wife was pregnant and was about to deliver the baby, she struck with labour pain. Citing this incident Gandhiji says, "Suddenly my wife started suffering from labour pain. There was no doctor and the midwife had to be called. I performed every thing regarding her labour. Fortunately, I had read *'Mane Shikhamana'* that was a book on this subject and because of that knowledge I did everything." This incident shows his power of taking decisions instantly. This is important for any management professional that he should develop a habit to take decisions instantly. It does not matter how adverse the situation is.

No to Precious Gift

When Gandhiji had to return India , he thought about the way to get rid of gifts he had been gifted there. He has accepted that he inspired others to say no to precious gifts and jewelry. Explaining his ideas about this matter he said, "May be I accept this. But what about my children? What about my wife? They had been taught to serve. They had been taught that service is priceless. I never kept precious jewelry and other such articles. Believe in simplicity was mounting every moment. In such a situation what was the worth of a golden watch? Who would wear those golden chains and rings? At that moment I also preached people to stay away of these things? Now what will I do with these articles?

I reached to a conclusion that I did not keep these things. He prepared a deed to make Rustamji as the trustee of these jewelry and decided to talk to his wife and children on this issue in the morning.

I was aware that it was tough to convince my wife and was confident to convince children. He decided to make his children his advocate in this matter."

The biggest quality in Mahatma Gandhi was that he followed everything himself before advising anybody to follow that. Following the ideals set by himself is an important quality of a successful manager.

Himself Acted as Scavenger

It was an incident of 1901, when Gandhiji went to Calcutta to address the Congrees Session. He was perplexed to see the conditions there. The management was worst. Everyone was passing his burden of duty to others. Regarding it Gandhiji writes, "There was no limit to garbage. There was water all around. Even today whenever I remember that scene I feel that stinking smell. I show the condition to one of the volunteers. He said angrily– 'This is not my job?' I asked for a broom. That volunteer was amazed. I found out a broom myself; cleared the night soils. But that was for convenience. There were so many people that this could have been cleared after every single use. This was beyond my capacity to do everything. That's why I also behaved like them for some time. I saw that no one was concerned about that.

It was not the limit. There were a lot of people who did not bother to go outside for the call of nature. None was willing to clear it. I achieved the glory of clearing all that."

Observance of Celibacy For Social Service

Gandhiji performed his duties with utmost dedication. At first he used to decide what to do for himself? And he executed that properly. When Gandhiji was living in Natal, South Africa, the 'Julu Mutiny' evoked. Julu was a community living in South Africa. Gandhiji found an opportunity to serve these people Julu people. When he vowed to social service, he decided to reduce the familial responsibilities. Considering this vow he decided to observe celibacy. He got this lesson during the his service to Julu community. In this regard Gandhiji says, "At this juncture the idea of celibacy became mature. I also discussed this with my friends. It is important to meet God to observe celibacy. I had not been able to experience it but I understood that it was important for the sense of service. I understood that through this I would be able to pay more time to serve others otherwise most of my time will be lost in maintaining the family affairs. There may not be a riding on two horses simultaneously. If my wife is pregnant, it is sure that I cannot devote my time in the service of others. Indulgence in the act of family multiplication and not observing celibacy, goes against the efforts of services to the society. Idea of observing celibacy even though being a married man would not annoy the relatives and society and this thought was fascinating me. I was anxious about it. Such ideas provided me joy and inspired me. Imagination has broadened my limits of services very much."

A successful management guru should always be prepared for any changes required for the fulfillment of the goal, if required.

Do not think any job inferior

Gandhiji never considered any job inferior. He implemented himself whatever he said on any topic. When he reached to Haridwar on the occasion of Kumbha, he felt that there were no proper system for cleaning. He decided to take the challenge himself. Describing this situation he wrote in his autobiography, "We have observed at Shanti Niketan that doing the job of a sweeper will be our special profession in India . The arrangement of tents were made for volunteers at the inn. There were small pits as lavatories. The arrangement for cleaning these pits at this occasion was possible only by him that can be done by the sweepers. Those pits should be kept covered and the pills of *phinix* should be put in them.

These suggestions were accepted by doctor Dev happily. I was one who demanded these services and Magan Lal Gandhi was one who was the bearer of these demanded services."

Compassion for the Poor

Once a leprous man reached to Gandhiji in South Africa. Initially Gandhiji wanted to send him quickly by providing something to eat, but later he took him in to his room. He washed his injuries and put medicines on those. But he could not be kept longer in the home, so Gandhiji sent him to the government hospital of Germatia. But this incident inspired Gandhiji to do something for such people. Doctor Booth Saint Adams was a officer in the 'Mission'. He had a lot of compassion and love for the poor and he distributed medicines among them freely. In his observance, Rustamji had opened a small hospital there. Gandhiji started serving such people in that hospital.

Respect for Elders

The incident of Gandhiji's first year's examination of high school is worth mentioning. The inspector of education department , Mr. Jailes, came to inspect. He asked the students of standard one to write five words. His first word was 'ketil'. Gandhiji wrote that incorrectly. The teacher tried to tell him the answer by indicating towards his shoes, but he ignored that. He could not understand that his teacher was trying to tell him the answer by showing the slate of the student opposite to him. All the students wrote correctly except Gandhiji. Later, the teacher told him his foolishness. But it had no impact upon him. He never imitated others. After all this he still had respect for the teacher in his heart. It was not his habit to look at the mistakes of elders since his childhood. Later on, he visualised numerous more mistakes in his teachers but his respect for the teacher always remained same. He knew that elders should be obeyed but should not be imitated.

If a man is asked to sweep the road he should do that in the similar way as Michal Angelo did his paintings or Beethovan composed his songs or Shakespeare wrote his poems. That road should be cleaned in such a way that every passer by stop there to praise the work done.

It is very important for a management guru to perform his job efficiently and with total dedication. There must not be any difference between words and deeds. He must be aware of his duties. He should not consider any job bigger or trivial. Because a successful management guru is one who becomes a role model for others. Gandhiji did every work with total dedication and honesty. He did work physically but accepted that at the mental level. In this chapter, whatever guidelines we find , we should draw inspiration out of that and try to imbibe them in our lives:

1. Be aware of your duties.
2. Do not consider any job trivial.
3. Do some change in your life style if required for achieving the goal.
4. Set an example for others by your sheer perserverance.

❑

6

Respect for Time and Labour

- *Even a single minute cannot be recovered. In spite of knowing it, we still lose our precious time.*
- *There is no karma greater than labour. It has magical power. Nothing can be done without complete honesty and dedication.*

–Mahatma Gandhi

Respect for Time and Labour

Time does not respect those who do not respect it. It is my belief that our daily routine should be designed in such a way that everything should be done properly. Gandhiji was aware of it and planned everything in a way that would be time for every activity. People used to say that one can match their time with his routine. He never altered his schedule for prayer. He managed his routine in such a way that he had time for every activity. He had said about his management:

- Those who save time will not indulge in silly affairs.
- Good act should be done promptly whereas bad ones must be avoided.
- Never postpone anything for tomorrow.

Gandhiji always respected the values of time. He was a perfect planner and executor. He laid down his daily routine in such a way that he had ample time for everything. Rarely there would have been any rescheduling of his daily routine. It is an example of his sheer practice of time bound routine that when he went to meet Lord Mountbatten at appropriate time he asked to leave because that was the time for his prayer.

For a successful management guru it is compulsory to follow strict time management. It is a fact that the time lost is never recovered at all. 'Time' is the key to success. Miscalculated timing can ruin all your plans. There are people who love to eat biscuit after dipping into tea. Mind here, that timing is all so important that every fraction of delay can cost you the taste of that dipped in tea biscuit. And if your timing is perfect, you can enjoy your quickly made dish. This is a great example that lays emphasis on the importance of timing and time management.

Many a time people miss their train by a second. They reach at station, witness the departure of train but cannot board it because they are late a few second. This is time when people realize the importance of few seconds. We have to spend time, money and labour to rectify our mistake. The mental stress associated with it is like bonus. That is why, it is elementary to understand the value of time to achieve success.

There are few workers who love delayed arrival at office, their boss always makes complaint about it. It may be possible that these people work more than those on time comers but still this delay factor furnishes the image in boss's eyes. So, be punctual first. Gandhiji is an ideal example of this. He was a craftsman of time management and this exemplifies that the man being so busy in various activities and movements had time for everything. If he can, why not we?

Importance of Labour

If you want to achieve a big success, you need to understand the pivotal importance of labour. The way Gandhiji accomplished everything throughout his life is worth following. Even at the time when his health deteriorated he never gave up his discipline and was always eager to do something that let the others keep guessing behind his perfect execution of time management. At the age of 78 the charisma, he was willing to travel Pakistan on his feet by road. There was a passionate and determined Gandhi who was able to produce such energy and zeal that made tough task easier. In his autobiography he himself writes, "It is very painful for me to remain alive with the help of friends and not doing anything."

There is a power within you that can elevate you to a greater position in comparison to your friends. If you want to climb to new height of success, what is needed is to accept the importance of labour. Gandhiji had always worshipped the labour during the lifetime. At the time when the country was facing the wrath of partition and Hindus and Muslims were killing one another, Gandhiji observed fast. He was in

78th years of his life. Still he converted it in such a determined way that rocked the nation. Above all it was a great example that establishes the importance of labour.

Gandhiji was of the opinion that if you want to provide support morally to your family and society, keep faith in labour. He never preached this unless he excelled this theory himself. From birth till death he kept himself active. Establishing the value of truth Gandhiji says, "Those who are devotees of truth and non-violence, who wants to serve India and mankind, cannot remain in inertia. One who losses time carelessly, destroys truth, non-violence and service.

If we take into account time, cleanliness etc. these will be no lack of knowledge. Actually what we call the lack of knowledge is lack of concentration and nothing else."

Gandhiji always emphasized on the importance of labour. He told that one could not understand the importance of labour of a man until he himself did it. That's why we say, "There cannot be anything noble and greater than doing labour for an hour daily just in a way the poor people have to do."

Gandhiji says that the labour not only keeps you fit but also provides satisfaction to the soul. There will not be any kind of thought that kindles a sense of guilt within that you do not deserve what you have been provided. There are many people in that world that spend sleepless nights. The reason of this is lack of concentration. Performing labour is very important for concentration. He says, " To develop power to concentrate to a high degree, it is needed to delve deep into the work you are doing. To make it better you strive hard constantly and this explores new height of concentration."

Gandhiji opined that the problem of poverty could not be mitigated until every citizen of India vowed to do labour unitedly. He writes in this context:

- The problem of poverty will be eliminated only if people of India denounce laziness.
- Laziness is the prime reason for India's poverty.
- Those who share other's burden cannot be an unemployed.
- Those who promote inertia in the name of destiny are criminals.
- It is important to put an effort to imbibe qualities.

For being a successful management guru, it must be vowed not to wish anything without executing appropriate labour for that. It is unbecoming of a human being if one doesnot work for their wishes. To get success, it is essential to adopt the importance of labour. So, acceptance of labour and practising it throughout the life is very important.

Let us draw inspiration from the life of 'Father of Nation' and imbibe those in our life right from this very moment.

- We have to draw plans for tomorrow's activities.
- Ponder on the fact that who is responsible for this disorganized routine.
- Do not waste even a minute.
- Do your work for yourself.
- Develop your personality in such a way that work is work. There is nothing like inferior or superior work.
- Do not deny to work.

❑

7

Positive Attitude

As common man knowing my limitation, I am happy with my service to my nation. Along with this, I always keep in mind that nobody should get hurt. It is impossible to be an international human being until you are not nationalist. Internationalism is possible only on the base of nationalism. It means when people from different countries organize themselves in such a way that they can work altogether. Nationalism is not a deemed theory provided that it should be away from selfishness.

Young India (part 2), page 129

Positive Attitude

Live the life to its fullest as long as you are alive. It is like embracing death before death if there is no zeal and excitement in life. Zeal and wish transform a common into a special. As the slight difference of temperature transforms water into steam and steam and drive any engine, in the same way curiosity drives us forward. This zeal can be kindled only through positive attitude. If you have positive attitude you can move towards the success even in adverse condition. But if you have a negative attitude, you are bound to loose your patience even at the time of smaller difficulties. This can create many enemies around you too. Positive attitude whereas can make your enemies your friend. There was a bright light of positive attitude within Gandhiji. He has kindled such a attitude of life within that illuminated his soul always. Love for mankind. Praising others, accepting mistakes, treating everybody equally etc. were his rare qualities that earned the glory of being the most dynamic persona of his time for him. He always fought for truth and opposed falsehood.

Equality

It is a story about a wise man who was sitting outside his village. A traveller passing by asked, "What kind of people live in this village because I am thinking to shift to this village?" That wise man asked , "What sort of the people of the village where you live?" The traveller replied, "They are selfish, inhuman and rude." The wise man said that the people in this village are the same. After sometime another traveller came and asked same question to wise man and wise man put up the similar question. The traveller replied, "People there are humble, kind and cooperative." The wise man assured him, "The people of this village are same."

The above narrated story points out that your attitude determines the way you look at the people. We can see the qualities in others if we have a positive attitude. And a negative attitude will force us to glare at others' drawback. Gandhiji always tried to see the society on the whole equally. He had the eyes through which he saw the people of entire globe equally. Once he had said, " There has been so many incidents that introduced me very closely with the people of different castes and religions. On the basis of these experiences, it can be said that I never know difference between own and others, countrymen or foreigners, white and black, Hindu , Muslim or Christian or Parsi or Yahudi."

I feel that Gandhiji was a spiritual man. How and in which condition he joined politics is different matter. Once a man said to Gandhiji that if you are truly spiritual, you should not join politics. You should meditate to reach the God. He smilingly replied that I was following the path which could reach to God. What is problem? He always respects his opponents. In this context he writes, "Humbleness means respecting your opponents, simple behavior, protecting their interest and behaving accordingly."

Gandhiji revered all religions similarly and accepted this publically. He was well aware of the fact that his acceptance might hurt few but he did not care about it because he himself established that truth is the purest form of religion. And that's why he once says, " I believe in Bible and Geeta equally. I believe that all the religions of this world are as true as my religion."

Not only Gandhiji reversed all religions equally but he emphasized that all religions were only the different paths to reach the Almighty. It does not matter which path you adopt when the ultimate destination is one. He opined,

"Considering one self's religion better than others' and asking other to justify act, it is the zenith of intolerance and intolerance is a kind of violence." It is because of this attitude of Mahatma Gandhi that Congress evolved as such a party which embraced people of all castes and religions. Gandhiji formulated a policy for keeping altogether and this became pivotal axis of the independence struggle. Gandhiji had said, "Unity does not mean only political unification. The real meaning is the unbreakable rapport between hearts. For this type of unity it is important for the Congress men to consider themselves the representatives of their religion whether it is Hindu, Muslim Christian, Parsi or Yahudi."

For success in the field of management, it is necessary that those who are interested in this field develop the kind of qualities that enables you to proceed with keeping all intents. Because if you achieve success to a great extent , you too march successful forward with the team not with an individual. Gandhiji has set ideal example in his life based on this. A management man can elevate his graph of success following Gandhiji's principles.

Faith on Others

The most successful businessman of this century Dhiru Bhai Ambani has said that if you want to become a successful industrialist, find out some reliable colleagues.

You cannot expand your business until you find out some reliable persons and believe on them. I believe that his statement was the result of the understanding of Gandhiji's philosophy of life because he found reliable colleagues and believed on them. In South Africa when he needed a typist he found a girl named Miss Sleshin who worked for him.

Gandhiji had said that sister was barely of seventeen years at that time. There was no any iota of vice in her. She expressed his views and ideas candidly before Gandhiji. Gandhiji said that her pure hurt always impressed me. I could understand his knowledge and understanding very well. In this context he had said, "I considered his knowledge in English was better than me and I believed her completely. And I used to sign papers typed by her without reading them most time."

Positive Attitude

William James of Howard university says, "The greatest research in my generation is that human being can make their life better by changing their attitude of life."

Gandhiji always adopted positive attitude and he was not only kept focus on achieving the goal but also means to achieve it. He said that the roots of the ideas must be positive. If the results are not as per your desire, there must be some other desire awaiting you. He worked in planned way to reach up to the goal. Along with this he was always prepared to accept failures if any and tried to find some positive outcome. That's why he had said, " I have seen mango time that results are against wishes. I have also observed that where truth is worshipped, we do not get unexpected results but whatever happens will be better than the expected one."

Gandhiji always emphasized that confluence of modern and ancient. Few people blame him as anti-modernist, but this is not so. He always opposed the evil things in the name of modernity. Once a man asked Gandhiji what was the difference between him and Nehruji. In reply, he said that Nehru ji opposed the British but loved Englishism whereas

I love British not Englishism. This was the example of his positive attitude that he welcomed every new scientific researches that mitigate the problem of common people. Commenting on the new initiatives in the field of education he said, "If this new system is really new it will fill hearts with new hopes instead of hopelessness , earn bread, generate employment, unite people and our children will learn how to read, write along with learning skill because through this they will learn alphabets."

There were three men moulding bricks. A traveller asked them what were you doing? The first man replied , "Don't you see that I am earning my livelihood?" The second said , "Don't you see I am moulding bricks?" The third one said, "I am building a beautiful building." Question was the same but answers were different. Now the question arises why is the difference? Is there effect of their attitude on their work ? The answer is crystal clear - 'Yes'. If the management has not positive attitude the result can never be positive.

Oppose the Superstition

Gandhiji always opposed superstition. He had firm faith the existence of God but he ridiculed such tradition that divided the society. He was the supporter of those traditions that promoted hinduism, at the same time he opposed the tradition of untouchability and *purda system* etc.

He made it clear that his opposition did not amount to denounce the religion. My intention was to abolish these superstitious traditions and establish an ideal character. Gandhiji also said, "I never believed in purda system. I believe that this custom is waning rapidly and those girls who have the courage to denounce these veils, can show their neighbors that there is no harm of it. Such girl will be most effective in eliminating the fear and prejudice regarding 'purda system'. Denouncing it does not mean girls can roam anywhere. I am talking about hiding their face which is detrimental to self improvement and self confidence of the girls. The best veil and defense is the girl's humbleness".

The aforesaid example makes it quite clear that broadening the ideas is pivotal for a management guru. He must process those qualities which enable him to oppose those evil forces that led to decline.

Welfare of all

The economic philosophy of Gandhiji was based upon his moral and humanitarian values. It was his opinion that the economic policy must be made upon the traits and capabilities of mankind. The economic policy must not be made for the benefit of few people and for the loss of most people.

Gandhiji always laid emphasis upon the welfare of all. He never tried to divide society on the basis of class. He told that all are Indian irrespective of caste religion or class. Hindus, Muslims, Parsi, Sikh, etc. are the people of this country. Their place of worship may be different but the temple like Inda is for all. People of all religions worship only one God His opinion reflects his positive attitude of the society. A successful management Guru must have to take into consideration that he must see the people of his work area with equal eyes. The co-operation of all will be helped achieving the target.

All work are important

Whatever you are doing must be done with dedication and commitment. Even the small work done with honesty and labour is bigger than the work done through fraudulent method.

Remember, you sacrifice your ego, and do everything by your hand, you make an impression upon your colleagues. Turn your thought into conduct. Your soul becomes fearless when you sacrifice your ego and hyprocrisy. When you agree with your work at mental level, the result will be 100% true. So, a management Guru must have to do any work with full potential.

Dedication Towards Improvement

Dedication towards improvement makes your soul free. You benefit not only present but also next generation by breaking the barriers of evil customs of society. Remember to end the evil just try for once, then see how many people come with you and motivate you. It is the theory of improvement. A good 'management' employee should always march for improvement.

Think not only Big, think Good

We get huge light and vision in our life in developing positive vision from the Gandhiji's policies and thoughts. He believed that positivity develops with good thought and work in good direction. In this context, his thoughts are as follows:

- True effort never goes in vain, true words do not.
- True effort never fails and at the end true words proves sweeter.
- People forget grief when they laugh, weeping increased the sorrows.
- Never hide the vices of others even though they are your relatives.
- One never get tired if he follows the ethics of life.

- One should go for human causes.
- Holy Ganga resides within human beings. He does not have a dip into it and remain empty.
- Maintain friendly relation with all in the world, this can change everything.
- It is to be justified that if someone attains completeness, everything is possible.
- It is important to think good rather than big.

❑

8

Devotion for Words

The decision of eatables is not based upon the rhymes of the scriptures but this has been developed freely with my life. I do not want to live as one who eats anything or getting treated just to remain alive. The religion that I have followed for my wife , children and beloved ones, how can I forget that when it is related to me.

–My Experiments with Truth P 414

Devotion for Words

Gandhiji's biggest power was inherent in his words. He tried to do whatever he told. He told that we should speak true, and he followed it in his life. He adopted Non-violence and Satyagraha as part of his personality and also adopted in his life. There is a speciality in Indian people and soil, it provides greater importance to them who leave rather than who receives. If a person proves that there is no difference between his words and efforts, then even today the whole country is ready to follow him. Gandhiji did not only recognise it but also cite an ideal example. He told that the people were the son of God, whom you thought untouchable. We should not make any partiality. He proved this with his conduct.

For a successful 'management' employee, it is important to have faith on others. He should use their words while considering the things. He should try to implement, as he had told. In this context Gandhiji himself said, "Not only the evil thoughts but disorganised and unwanted thoughts that come into mind are destined to dent your power consistently. We ramain unaware of this. As thought inspires words and deeds, it is always true that your act and words will be as per your thought. That's why a thoroughly evolved idea is the most powerful and it may be possible you start doing desired things without any external help.

There are lot of inspiring incidents in Gandhiji's life, it shows that he did whatering he told. He told that in a way of truth we had have a power with which we could move towards the height of life. He said about truth, "Truth is a big tree. It bears fruits as it is nursed. There is no end of it."

Thought About Non-Violence

Gandhiji followed his words as he told others to follow. There will not be even a drop of blood-shedding in the world today if we understand the ideas of non-violence of Gandhiji. We remember Gandhiji when common people died in a terrorist activity or blast.Consider that one kills other. Rather kills the former. Again getting a chance the former attacked the acquaintances of the latter. If this is followed across the globe, the world will be changed. There will only be rivers of blood. That's why, leaving aside these differences, we should employ and celebrate brotherhood and co-operation. This is easy to say but hard to follow. In this context Gandhiji said, "The path of non-violence is not an easy one, but it is permanent and good for both.This has been a tradition to kill in revenge of killing. But this has not been able to provide peace and eliminate injustice and exploitation from the world. My experience says that the only key to it is non-violence."

Gandhiji always loved the nation more than anything. These are not empty words but there are so many examples during his life that establisehs these words as true. He strived to do his best to stop the division of the nation. When Novakahli was burning in the fire of riots, Gandhiji went there bare-footed. He used to say, "I love my country more than my body."

Gandhiji understood the secret that for development in life one had to develop his internal qualities. There was a need to part the differences between words and deeds. One had to be conscious about his words. He believed that aforesaid guidance if followed, there would be automatically for all sorts of problems. That's why he said, "Wealth is not money on the end, but the patience, truth, efficiency and faith."

For becoming a successful management guru it is mandatory to develop above qualities in their personality. If he is able to develop these aforesaid qualities, success will kiss his feet and he will be able to achieve his aims targeted.

Dedication for Truth

During the law practice in Johanesburg, Gandhiji vowed not to advocate false cases. Everybody, knew this and never went to him with a false case. Once Gandhiji was advocating a case. During the course of hearings he got to know that the young man, for whom he was advocating, had cheated him. Immediately Gandhiji requested the Magistrate to reject the case. The opponent advocate was surprised at this but the Magistrate was happy. This following of truth enhanced his respect all the more. Gandhiji believed that we should follow our words at any cost; no matter what the cost was. The final result of truth remained always good, he opined always. Describing the importance of dedication for the words, he said –

- Even if one word of truth is enough. Lying is always unfruitful.
- Silence is less harmful than much speaking.
- There is no joy like truth and no sorrow like lie.
- Nothing is possible until there is a co-ordination between body, mind and soul.

❑

9

Constant Development of Abilities

The end of a 'Satyagraha' is possible only when there is more vigour evident among people."

My Experiments with Truth, P. 404.

Constant Development of Abilities

"Being unaware of anything is not shameful, but it is the state of denial to learn that."

It is very important for a successful management employee to enhance his abilities consistently. Because there is none who is perfect. But those who are eager to learn move towards perfection. I remember that once a grammarian told two of his students that their pronunciation was not good. Instead of 'Sh' you pronounced 'S'. Apart from this, there are many problems also. He said that I felt you should practice to correct it. One of the students considered it seriously. He said that I would try seriously. He asked the problem in his pronunciation. The other one said that others could understand his words. Both the students met their guru after six months. One had rectified his pronunciation upto 80% whereas the other was as he was earlier.

What do you feel? There is only one difference between them. The former wanted to develop his skills and abilities. He wanted to amend his mistakes. The latter had no such wish. The result was that the former induced towards perfection but the latter was constant where he was. If we want to develop our abilities, we need to develop it consistently no matter you belong to industrial sector or service sector.

Gandhiji developed his abilities consistently. When you have a glance at his childhood, you can see he was eager to learn new things since that time. He never considered any work trivial. Whenever he felt that certain work had to be done and there was none to do that, he did those without any hesitation. Mentioning an incident he writes in his autobiography — "Once I went to a barber's shop in Pretoria. He denied to serve me and ridiculed me also. I felt sorry. I went to market and bought a hair-cutting machine. I returned home and cut my hair myself standing before the mirror. It was difficult but I managed to cut my hairs in someway. But the cutting was uneven. When I reached court, all burst into laughter."

A successful management should acknowledge the fact that there is nothing like trivial affair or job, but at time he should accomplish all sort of works to realize his dream.

Emphasis on the development of Internal Power

Gandhiji was of the opinion that if one had to enhance his abilities, development of internal powers was mandatory. For this, we should gain experience supported by vast reading. He believed that it was impossible to achieve the set target unless you develop your internal powers to its fullest. That's why he said, "Value of human depends upon their behavior not on their post. This behavior cannot be judged on the basis of external life. This can only be ascertained knowing the internal ingredients."

Life is just like a ten-geared cycle. Most of us have such gears that we never use.

There are very few people who utilize even the 20% of their total capacity. Most of people use only 10-12% of their god-gifted ability. Because they neither wish to achieve something in life nor have any urge to learn new things. Gandhiji adopted this in his life. Whatever Gandhiji imbibed in his life, that was not for few moments but became eternal part of his life. We do not gain perfection in anything because we do not practice that again and again. Once the great violin player Fritz Krisller was asked, "How do you play violin so beautifully? You are fortunate?" He replied, "It is possible only because of practice if I do not practice it for a month, my audience can feel the differnce. If I do not practice for a week my wife can tell the difference. And if I miss the practice even for a day I can tell the difference." Gandhiji followed every norm that he formulated for himself be it prayer or anything else. He was of the opinion that any movement launched by him was not important because it started, for him the importance of that lies in the fact that at the end of the movement how many people agree to it. He said, "The final end of the Satyagraha will be at the time when more vigorous force will be evident among people at the end of it."

Development of abilities is important for being a successful management employee. For this an urge to learn and constant practice of those things that we want to imbibe in our life are important. Gandhiji is an ideal in this regard. Let us implement these things in our life from today onwards.

1) Develop your abilities consistently
2) Accept your mistakes and find their solutions.
3) Use all your abilities to clinch your goal.

❑

10

Do the Work in Organized Manner

"The feeling to do good work is itself an award. It is better to do few good works rather than so many things in a bad way."

–Mahatma Gandhi

Do the Work in an Organised Way

"I can provide you a certificate that there might be any word that comes at of my tongue or pen without properly thinking about that. I do not remember any speech or article for which I had to apologise. On the contrary in same we from many dangers. And so much of time saved was dividend."

Inscribing these words in his autobiography, Mahatma Gandhi had the art to organise his routine and work in such a way that establishes him as a successful management guru of 20th century. In the field of commerce, a lot of employees remain connected with the objective of the organisation. It is important to regulate your tongue and thought for the desired success of your organisation. Gandhiji proved through his ideas and principles that we could achieve success by organising our work. Along with using the avoidable resources, reaching to the aim is also efficient management. Gandhiji has set an example through his working style. That is why he was an expert in the field of management.

Emphasis on Discipline

Gandhiji always emphasized to observe discipline to accomplish his task efficiently. He believed that we cannot achieve our goal in an organized way until we observe strict discipline. He had accepted discipline as an important instrument for success in the life. In this context, he said, "Teacher can tell the student about only those paths which are best in his eyes or in the state's. After doing this, they have no right to suppress the ideas and emotions of students. It does not mean that there should not be any discipline. No any school can run without discipline. But I do not consider artificial code of disciplines good for the overall development of the students."

Today it is very important for a management man to observe strict discipline in organising his works. Because along with enhancing his capacities, the outcome happens to be positive and impressive.

Sharpen Your Intellect

There was a woodman named John, was working in a company for five years. During these years there was no any increment. On the other hand Bill, the other woodman, got increments within a year. John felt hurt when he knew this and went to urge the owner. The owner replied, "You still are cutting only the same number of trees as five years back. We want better workers in our company. If you can enhance your output I will be happy to increase your salary." John went back and devoted more time in tree cutting but the output did not increase as expected. Being disappointed he told his problem to the owner. The owner advised him to consult Bill and said, "It may be possible that we know something that you do not." John asked Bill the secret of his efficiency. Bill replied, "After cutting each tree, I sharpen my axe for two-three minutes. Tell me when did you sharpen your axe?" This question of Bill opened the eyes of John and he got his solution.

The above story teaches us that you can not get desired results if you do not plan that properly. Through his organized abilities Gandhiji had said that it was possible to do multi-tasks altogether. He never considered any job trivial. He was of the opinion that we should do whatever we do with our heart. Thus, he said, "Feeling good for doing anything is the biggest award. It is better to do few good works rather than bad." Let us implement few of the elements of the life of Gandhiji in our life from today onwards:

1. Do your job with proper planning.
2. It is not only important to accomplish the task, it is equally important to accomplish it in a proper manner.
3. Discipline must be followed all the time.

❑

11

Inspiring Others

Mahatma Gandhi was supporter of simple marriage. Jamnalal Bajaj was like his son. Generally being rich, Marwaris spend extravagantly in their marriages. But with the inspiration of Gandhiji Jamanalal arranged the marriage of his daughter, Kamala with a student of Gujarat Vidya peeth, Rameshwar Newaria in the simplest way.

–Vijay Joshi

Inspiring Others

The simplicity of Gandhian philosophy is rare in the world. Gandhiji applied his ideals on himself first and then made those very practical. He included humanism, love, truth, non-violence, welfare , equality and spirituality that popularized his ideas vastly.

Arindam Choudhary,a noted economist, expresses his ideas about Gandhiji, "Gandhiji and Lord Krishna are the two important sources of inspiration for us." Describing the popularity of Gandhiji, Dominique Leperrie and Larry Collins say, "The man lying in the hut smearing with cowdung was very lean and thin. This man of 77 years, whose face was smiling under the bag of wet soil, rocked the roots of the British Empire. That old man was keen to introduce a new era. It was this old man who forced the Prime Minister of an Empire that never saw sunset in their vast Empire to find a way for Indian independence. Thus, he was ot an ordinary man but was determined to abolish the British Empire."

In the book *'Gandhi Marg'* written in Gujrati, Acharya Kriplani writes, "Gandhiji became a saint only because of the fact that he inspired millions of people with his life, ideas, principles and ideals." Gandhiji had said, "The solution of my philosophy is in my ideas. You can't say it Gandhism."

The ideas expand rapidly. Gandhiji had an amazing personality. On one hand, he was the reason of biggest worry for the British. On the other hand, he became the supreme hero of the freedom fight for the Indians. He established such a rapport with the common people of the nation that was almost impossible to imagine. Millions of people followed his call promptly. People were eager to spend all they had with just one call of Mahatma Gandhi. It was his efficient management skill that he established rapport with the common people of the nation as well as with the media also.

It is very important for a management guru not only to impress others with their works but also inspire others to follow him. There are many incidents in the life of Gandhiji that inspired millions of people of the nation. Winston Churchill, Bernard Shaw, Leo Tolstoy and Bettard Russel. Few of those eminent personalities were inspired by Gandhiji . at the time of Gandhiji's demise Russels said, " Gandhiji was the compound of Jesus and Abraham Lincon." Such was the impact of Gandhiji that he was famous worldwide.

Some incidents worth noting

Gandhiji has mentioned some incidents in his autobiography that reflects his ability to impress and inspire the others. When he launched struggle in South Africa, a lot of the Blacks as well as the white were inspired with him. Describing it he notes that few of the white men stood with me with whom I had spent time in Britain. He mentions in his biography that when he was in Britain he lived like them. But when they came with me the situation changed. He writes, "At that time I lived the way they lived. My stay there was just like a stay in a hotel. Here the thing was opposite. They became like my relatives. Many a time they followed the Indian way of lifestyle. Even the architect and furnishings were of English style still the lifestyle and food habits were very much Indian. I remember that there were few problems with them. But I can say that both were mingled with each other."

When Gandhiji arrived South Africa and waged the war he needed companions. With increasing work load he was in need of someone who can act as a clerk as well as can share his work load. He found miss Dik, about whom he writes, "She became not only my clerk but also I believe that she became just like my own daughter or sister. I had never to scold her. There were rare mistakes in her work. There was a time when she managed the transaction of thousands of Euros and kept the accounts herself. She won my confidence completely and I was also able to clinch a confidence in her that she believed me similarly. She asked my opinion to select her life partner. I was fortunate to perform *'kanyadan'* for her. It was obvious that when miss Dik became Mrs. Mac Donald , she should have parted her way, but she was always available at my call in my needs."

Once Gandhiji was asked by someone what was the difference between you and Nehru? He replied, "Nehru opposes British and loves Britishism. Whereas I love British and opposes Britishism." There was a vast experience behind this statement. During his initial years of life whether it was in England or South Africa, he understood the fact that there was nothing like good or bad, caste or race. Individuals happen to be good or bad. During his life time, he experienced a lot of human qualities in various English men with whom he worked. Even there were many British who were impressed with him. There was another English woman whom Gandhiji rated more than his group of companions. Gandhiji said to one of her friends about her, "So much of selflessness, purity, fearlessness and such efficiency were rarely seen in people. In my opinion, Mrs. Saleshin is the best among your friends."

There was another English man that stood with Gandhiji. He was impressed with this saint of India. He supported Gandhiji at his best during the struggle launched by Gandhiji in South Africa. Gandhiji writes about him , "He was my companion of all seasons during my stay in South Africa. I always knew Mr. Waist as a man who was born in a farmer's family, a student of common school, enriched with the self experience, composed, an ardent devotee, fearless and philanthropist English man."

Gandhiji inspired and impressed people across the sections. From common people to the politicians, workers to the industrialists and the social workers. All sections of the society were following the Father of Nation. Ghanshyam Das Birla and Jamana Lal Bajaj were few of his close associates. During the riots in the country when Gandhiji returned from Calcutta, he accepted to stay in the house that belonged to Birla. In this context, Dominique Leperrie and Lorry Edilins write, "The owner of that house, Ghanshyam Das Birla, was one of the two biggest industrialist families. They were the richest and their business included cotton mills, insurance ventures, banks and the factories of rubber, jute etc. He was one of the earliest disciples of Gandhiji still he launched first strike in his mill."

When you start establishing ideals before the society , a lot of people start following that. Beinjamin Franklin has said, "when you became good for others it is even better for you."

Once a child of ten years went to ice cream parlour and asked the waiter, "What is the price of a cone ice cream?" The waiter replied, " 75 cents". The child started counting the coins in his hand. He again asked the price of a smaller cone. The waiter replied angrily, "Sixty five cents". The boy said, "Give me that smaller one." He took the ice cream and paid the price. When the waiter went to bring the empty plate he was touched at whatever he saw. There were ten cents kept there as tip for him. That small kid considered about the waiter also. He showed compassion. He preferred others to himself.

There was a lot of compassion in Gandhiji. He connected himself with a lot of moral stories, plays and literature and other such means. I am citing one of his favorite stories:

An incident that impressed Gandhiji

A war was fought between the Arabs and the Romans after the death of Muhammad Saheb. A lot of soldiers died and many injured. At the evening it was customary to stop war. Once, when the war stopped in the evening an Arab soldier went to search his cousin. He was thinking that if body might recovered that would be buried and if he found living he would serve him. He took some water with him thinking that he might be thirsty. Holding a lamp in his hand he was moving ahead in search of his cousin through the area where soldiers were crying with the pain. He found his cousin who was dying for water. The injuried were bleeding . There was very grim hope of his survival. He kept the water mug beside him. Suddenly someone else cried for water. That kind soldier said to his brother, "Please give water to that soldier first". The soldier's brother rapidly went into the direction from which the voice was coming.

That injured man was an official of higher ranks. The said man was about to drink water, suddenly a cry was heard from the third direction. This officer was as kind as the earlier soldier. Thus, he managed to express his way in gestures to provide water to the third person first. The man rushed with water to that third man. But the man lost his life before he could reach. He did not get water. The man returned to the officer, but he also had stopped breathing. Sadly when he reached to his cousin he found that his cousin was no more.

None of the three could get water but the first two became immortal. There are so many stories inscribed in the pages of history. But this one is just to kindle realization within you so imbibe that quality to provide life and necessities at the cost of yourself. We should observe these ideals even at the cost of our life. This story inspired Gandhiji to serve the society.

In multi-linguistic and multi-cultural society, love, compassion and co-operation is important. Knowing each other's religion develops a better understanding and this is good for the society on the whole. Not keeping any bias against learning anything is an act of welfare for us. Better learning enhances the knowledge and makes attitude generous. There is nothing more beneficial than keeping your eyes and mind open.

Stopped Violence Alone

It is very important for a successful management guru to develop a kind of power within that everybody around him get inspired by him and try to follow him as well. Expansion of thought and transparency in his lifestyle made Gandhiji such a person that people never hesitated to follow him at all. At a time when the entire Calcutta was burning in the fire of riots, Gandhiji went there and put his efforts to stop violence. This is an exceptional example of influence. The number of attendants rose day-by-day which reflects his impact and acceptance in the society. On one hand, the violence was increasing constantly in Punjab and on the other hand people of Calcutta showed patience because of the efforts of Gandhiji. Citing this incident Dominique Leperrie Lapier and Lorry Collins write, "This time around one million people were looking the way of Gandhiji. At a time of unstoppable violence in Punjab, Gandhiji organized prayer every evening in Calcutta and surprisingly the number of people was increasing day-by-day. And this prayer brought peace and harmony in a city where ever growing and had taken the entire city into its grip. The violent people of this city heard the words of that votary of peace and controlled their ever growing hatred and violence in their hearts. This miracle at Calcutta is still alive. Like the New York times writes– "This city is magical in India."[5]

Gandhiji had said following about accomplishing the tasks efficiently:

- Our principles are tested even during the small affairs.
- There is not even a moment in the life when people can't serve.
- Life without ideals is just like a life of an animal.

❑

12

Setting and Achieving Goals

This time the magic at Calcutta was true and enduring. There was a fear of worsening conditions in the fields of Punjab, Karachi, Lahore and Delhi , but the city of fearful nights Calcutta kept its promise to Gandhiji. After that there was not even a drop of blood fell on the roads of Calcutta. His old friend Rajgopalachari said, "Gandhiji has accomplished many tasks but the way he won over vices was incomparable, there was not anything like that not even freedom.

–Freedom at Midnight P 336

Setting and Achieving Goals

"If there will not be a goal in the life and a definite way to follow then life will become just like a boat without helm. The greatest goal of life is to serve the people and take part in their betterment. This includes the true prayer and devotion of God. Those who act for God are called angels."

Gandhiji always emphasized that there must be a certain goal in the life and there must be a consistent effort to achieve that. Life without goal is like a boat without helm. Once goal is set, it is also important to gather the resources that can drive you to the goal and use them in the best possible way. The ability and capacity factors must be kept in mind before setting goals. If we did not understand abilities properly and set a goal that is not possible to achieve then one has to face depression and failure. That's why, it is important to have a proper knowledge about the area you are ascertaining your aim of life. When Gandhiji entered in to the political arena of india he was well aware of the conditions of the nation. He had understood the fact that Indians were not violent in their basic nature. He also thought that the country was not in a position to confront the alien ruler directly. For this, the need was to unite the segregated society into one unit.

Based on the above thoughts, he set a goal and chose the resources to achieve it. This goal made him a subject of surprise not only for the British but for the entire world. As to click a photo focus is required, similarly we should use our resources and policies efficiently to achieve our aim.

Napoleon Hill had written, "Human being can achieve anything that he can imagine and believe." Inspiration to achieve the goal is an outcome of strong will power.

There was a strong will power within Gandhiji to achieve his goal. He always tried to do things in a way he thought to do. The biggest quality of Gandhiji was the ability to judge the situation perfectly and taking decisions on the humanitarian grounds. On March 12, 1930 when this man marched towards Dandi from Sabarmati Ashram with his 76 followers, none had ever thought that this man would be able to create a wave across the nation and millions of people would follow him. But Gandhiji was confident of the outcome of that historic journey right from the beginning. And this was witnessed by the whole nation. This was the power of his policies, ideals and faith.

There was a historic agreement between Lord Irvin and Gandhiji on March 4, 1931. There had been rounds of talk to finalize the final drafting of the agreement and the results once again proved Gandhiji's ideals to reach to the goal. It has been said about this context, "There were eight meetings during a week and the result was termed famously as 'Gandhi-Irvin Pact'. Going through this pact it seems that this is an agreement between two equal powers and this indicates that it was the biggest victory of Gandhiji."

A successful management guru should set a clear goal. After that collect required information, broaden social and business base to gain power. We should use resources in the best possible manner to crack the target. To achieve the goal, it is important to repeat the good work done again and again. Gandhiji launched movement after movement and this enabled him to move towards his goal consistently. Along with this, his acceptance among Indian common people was ever growing.

Aim to Unite the Society

Gandhiji felt the thing very clearly that it was important to unite the Indian people socially for the political unification of the nation. He was well aware of the fact that the social division would always hamper the prospect to show our unity before the English ruler. That is why he stressed the need to unite the society first. For this he used his broadened ideals. Gandhiji knew that there were few fundamentalists who could be angry at this , but Gandhiji prioritized the aim.

Gandhiji did not hesitate a bit to ridicule the fundamentalism and the ideas of differentiation prevailed in the society at that time. He was Hindu still he targeted many inhuman traditions and expressed his ideas at broadened levels. He said, "Untouchability prevails in Hinduism only. There is neither any relation with intellect nor any evidence in the sacred scriptures. What I have read in the sacred scriptures and learned people have told me. I can conclude that there is no any evidence or basis for untouchability in Hinduism. Now I have neither time to look for what is written in the scriptures or what is not necessary to produce evidences in support of this. The important thing is that if you consider untouchability as a mark of shame on the face of Hinduism, there is an urgent need to put efforts to abolish it."

Gandhiji emphasized that we should do from the bottom of the heart whatever we do. If we are prepared only physically and not mentally the results would be disaster. That's why, in the context of this untouchability he said that we should denounce it from our souls and observe equality at all levels. He has said, "It will not be enough to start touching those who were untouchables earlier. But there is a greater meaning of this. The actual meaning of this is to abolish all sorts of differences."

For a successful management guru, it is very important to set a goal and strive to reach there. It is not only important to reach at the desired goal but along with it is also important that means and mental acceptability remains there.

Ability to take Decisions

Goal without action is just like empty dreams. Action transforms dreams into goal. If we did not achieve success it did not amount to failure. Delay does not mean failure, the only meaning of it is that there is a need to draw plans once again.

Gandhiji has established that he has the power to take right decisions at right time. When he reached Champaran in support of the workers, he made it clear to the Viceroy that his motive was not to instigate the workers but to solve the problems of these workers peacefully. If he would not have taken this decision, he might have been arrested and sentenced to death. Gandhiji was totally aware of the fact that Champaran movement was his first step on the Indian soil and that's why he was very cautious in the decisions regarding this movement. The first step should be taken in the state of complete clarity of ideas.

Contrary to it, when he launched 'Quit India Movement' on August 9, 1942 the aim and tone had been changed. Gandhiji knew it very well that the British government had not the answer to the way Indian people had united themselves to follow him. And he launched the movement with a slogan *'Do Or Die'* as the final war of independence. He had said, "Every Indian will take part in this movement as a General. It does not matter whether there is anyone of the working committee alive to advise and guide the movement, every Indian has to fight till death considering it the last war of independence and we have to win."

The above incident proves that Gandhiji took severe decisions at the time of need and used strong words too. But he always waited till the opportune time and conditions arrived. Once the time arrived when Gandhiji warned the British government in context of the Indian freedom and said, " I neither need wealth and honour nor the state of India, I want only the freedom of India."

The most important task for a successful management guru is to take right decisions at right time to achieve the goal. Being failed at once does not mean that you stop trying. Instead it is more important to strive harder. You are well aware of Abraham Lincon. He stated business at the age of 21, failed; at 22 lost the election, at 24 again failed in the business, lost his wife at 26, lost his mental balace at 27, at 34, lost the election of Congress, in 45th year of life he lost the election of Senate, at 47, he failed to become the Vice President, at 49, again lost the election of Senate and finally at the age of 52, he became the proud President of the USA.

Whenever we set the goal two things are very imporatant; one is circumstances and other is preparation. Preparations are like wind that can not be controlled but our preparation is like that of the instrument of boat that changes the direction of wind as per required and we have ourselves to determine the direction. It does not matter what the situation is. We need to fight against those and strive for our goals. Gandhiji had established the ideals that how to formulate policies at adverse times.

If we implement his policies in the field of management there will be sure success. If someone wants to achieve greater success in life, maturity and clear understanding is necessary. It means avoid being indulged in to trivial matters. Gandhiji was the best example of this.

Formulation of Correct Policy

Will you be willing to board a bus or train about whom you are not knowing where is it going? The clear answer will be– 'No'. You do not want to board such a bus or train and still living your life without any goal? For working in any field the target should be ascertained and then it should be strived to achieve. Gandhiji always emphasised this fact. That's why, he always said to the people of India during the national movement that the fight was not against the workers of the British government but the fight is against the policy of draining the resources of India to England.

Gandhiji felt that it is important for the complete solution of the problem to reach upto its root cause. That is why, when he launched the movement to boycott the foreign clothes the impact was visible on the mills in England. He linked the spinning wheel with the freedom struggle as a symbol and that was very surprising. Gandhiji always formulated policies for the goals and thus he was able to challenge the mighty British Government with very little resources.

If we formulate a clear policy then the journey to success becomes easy. There is an old story which tells us that there was a demon , who used to harass the people of the village. Once a young shepherd came to meet his brothers. He asked, "Why do not you fight with the demon?". The brothers were very afraid. He replied, "Do not you see he is so big that can not be killed?" Then he replied that if he is bigger then it is a matter of happiness because when we would hit him, we would not miss any. This is an example of right policy for the goal. Gandhiji always worked with this thinking and achieved his goals. This is also important for a management guru to think like this and draw policies accordingly.

Emphasis on Practicality

Gandhiji was the leader of people who fought by adopting truth and non-violence. During this struggle, the principle, amending policies and morality etc of the Gandhian principles are evident. But Gandhiji always emphasised upon the need to make every principle practical as much as possible. Gandhiji put an emphasis on the assimilation of ancient with the modern that was very friendly for the development of Indian villages. Gandhiji tested his ideals and principles regularly. That is why, all his experiments were successful. There was no any other example of politician of that era who was as potent speaker as Gandhiji.

To stop riots in Calcutta when he said , "Today the key of peace to the entire nation remains in the hands of Calcutta. The cosequence of even a small incidence can not be ascertained. If this fire extends to the villages it will be your responsibility to maintain calm in Calcutta."

His words had great impact on the common people. The people of Calcutta felt that if Gandhiji was saying that means were something dangerous and the consequences might be very ill fated. They felt to remain calm and obeyed Gandhiji's instructions. Because Gandhiji was well aware of the fact that once you would start moving towards the goal , people would follow you. For this, media was not required because everyone wanted to help the great cause.

A management guru can learn the art of management and the required things to achieve success from Gandhiji. One can draw inspiration from Gandhiji's life. Following things should be kept in mind while formulating your principles.

1. Set your goal after a thorough thinking.
2. Associate people who are needed to accomplish the task with you.
3. Develop the quality to take instant decisions.
4. Draw right policies to achieve success.
5. Emphasize the need of practicality.

❑

13

Best Use of Resource

He used to manage his routine with the help of a sixteen years old 'Ingersol' watch. There were very few things that he could say his own in which this watch was one. It was always hanging at his waist bound with a thread. He used to read Geeta at 2 o'clock in the night and prayed early in the morning. After that he would sit and reply the letters. He used the pencils as long as he was able to hold that because he said that the pencil was an outcome of the labour of a man like him and to destroy that would amount to disrespect for him.

–Freedom at Midnight P 65

Best use of Resources

It is a truth that life is a competition and we all are participating in it. Competition makes the competitors better. We can win only in a situation when we use our resources in the best possible way. It is important for a successful management guru to use his resources at its best, so that in a comparatively less time and expenditure the goal can be achieved.

If there is a target before us, we should strive hard not only 100% but upto 200%. Gandhiji never lost his patience. He adopted fast as the means to achieve his desired goal. Many a time, he made the society to realise his ideas through his fast. Accepting the fact, he said that his religion told him to observe fast and pray when the problem became unbearable many a time we think that small affairs do not harm us but Gandhiji himself believed that the impact of personality was adjudged through these small affairs.

There was a man walking on the sea beach in the morning. He saw that a lot of starfishes came at the shore with tides but they remained at the shore when the tides went back and they died of sun light. The tide were fresh and the starfishes were alive, That man moved for and picked a fish and threw that into water. He repeated that many times. There was a man standing behind him who was unable to understand it. He went near to him and asked, "What are you doing? There are hundreds of fishes in fact. How many of them will you save? The former did not reply, went few steps forward, picked fish and threw that into water and said, "It matters for this one fish."

Gandhiji always underlined the fact that these small things elevated human being to the great extent of greatness. That is why a management employee should focus on the best use of available resources rather than looking for more resources.

Self Confidence

A boy was drowning into the river. He screamed for help. A man who was passing by jumped into the river and saved the boy. When the man was about to go the boy said, "Thanks". That man asked, "For what?" The boy replied, "To save my life." That man saw in the eyes of the boy and said, "Son, when you get older remember that your life was worth saving." It is important for us to believe on our policies nad abilities. We should be proud of the fact that God has provided us the powers that differentiate us from other creatures. We can be successful by using our abilities at its best. We should be proud of ourselves and be confident. It is very simple that if we are not proud of ourselves how can be others. It is important to note here that we should not appreciate ourselves before others, let this for others , but we should feel it within our soul. If you appreciate yourself in front of others you will be considered as arrogant.

Gandhiji had tremendous self confidence. That is why, when he went to meet the King of England , he had donned the normal day dress. Describing his self confidence Dominique Lepperie and Lorry Collins had said, "After six months, the entire England was surprised to see that Mahatma Gandhi has come to meet the King in just a tiny piece of cloth and sleepers at Buckingham Palace. He was very much like the character of of the famous poet of English Rudyard Kipling's Gangadin, "That is in front is nothing and that is behind less than the half." Later on he was asked, "Was it appropriate to go there in that dress?" Gandhiji replied, "The king had donned so of the dress that it was enough for both of us."

Our confidence , determination and right use of resources lead us to the right path. It leads us towards the aim. Gandhiji was the embodiment of self-confidence and determination. He did whatever he determined to do at any cost. A management employee should also have such determination. Drawing inspiration from Gandhiji we should imbibe following things in our life immediately;

1. Best use of available resources.
2. Beaming self confidence.
3. Try to do every thing at least cost and less time.

❑

14

Remain Balanced in Adverse Circumstances

The real India is one that belongs not only to the Hindus but also to the Muslims, Sikhs, Parsis, and Christians. The real Pakistan is also one where all communities can exist happily and there will not be any hatred for any community.

–Prayer-preaching 1, Page 28-29

Remain Balanced in Adverse Circumstances

We need to learn from nature. The way duck swims in water very fast but remains calm and composed all the time. It is very important for a management employee to remain calm even in the adverse situation. A management employee has to maintain co-ordination among the people of different groups, different mental status while taking decisions for the organization. During the course of maintaining this balance there occurs many opposite situations. These situations are the testing times. He should take decisions with utmost care to be successful in this test.

Gandhiji led numerous movements during his life and worked with people of different mentality. But he had achieved patience in the form of mental peace that enhanced his power and efficiency all the more. Everyone has definite time for the accomplishment of a work and he has to finish that within time frame. If you lose much of your time in gossiping and other unproductive affairs then you will not have the sufficient time for the needed work or you may not perform it very well. So, it is important that such unproductive affairs and such people who keep you indulged you in such affairs must be avoided. In this context, Cyrus Chig has said, " I have learnt long before that do not wrestle with a pig. You will be muddled and this will make the pig happy." That's why for being a successful management guru it is required to remain calm in adverse situations and avoid unimportant matters. Gandhiji adopted this theory throughout his life and proved it through his policies. He has said about non-violence, "The real touchstone to adjudge non-violence is to remain non-violent in ideas, policies and act even at the time when your aggression for violence is at the top. It is not a big matter to remain non-violent before the well natured and well behaved people. Non-violence is the mightiest power of the globe that can stand against any greedy power."

There had been a lot of such occasions when Gandhiji was discriminated on the basis of colour, caste or language. But he never lost his temper. Describing the incident between him and the representative of 'Daily Telegraph', Mr. Eller Thorpe he writes in his autobiography, " I went to Calcutta. He was not aware of the fact that Indians were not allowed to stay in the deewankhana of a hotel. He knew it later. So, he took me in his own room. He was very sorry to see the uncultured behavior of the local English men towards Indians. He begged pardon for being not able to arrange a stay in the diwankhana."

Debate does not mean that the right things will be said at right time but also those things should be avoided that are not necessary. Gandhiji never said any such thing that endangered the communal fabric or spread hatred. He emphasized to maintain humanism and peace in the most adverse situations. There were times when few people were afraid that Gandhiji's statement can make few of the fundamentalists annoyed, but he never cared for them and stood by with humanism. When the revolutionary forces were applying violence to express their anger Gandhiji said, "Exploding bombs have harmed the cause of the independence. Those who have used arms in the name of Islam have denigrated their religion. If government loses its patience and uses force then it will be an act of foolishness. If it is sensible then it can understand that it is they who are responsible for these explosions. Denying the popular demand constantly the government has forced the people to lose their patience. And this has led few of us on the path of violence."

For a management guru, it is important to remain composed in the most adverse situations. Keeping an eye on the developments he should implement his decisions in such a way that there should not be any hurdle in the path of success.

In the context of maintaining calm at the adverse time Gandhiji said:

- Dedication is judged at the time of crisis.
- Inspiration is handicapped if mind is not supporting it.
- That who loses calm loses truth and non-violence.
- Why do people become impatient when he is not able to work?
- Illusion and truth can not march together.

❑

15

Transparency in Public Life

- *I Interrupted and said, "Abdullla Seth, the matter of my fee should not be raised. What kind of fee in the public service? If I will stay that can only be as a servant.*

  –My Experiments with Truth, Page 140

- *Personal gifts are prohibited in public life.*

  –My Experiments with truth, Page 214

Transparency in public life

When Gandhiji was about to return to India, a lot of people in South Africa presented him precious gifts. There were gold and diamond jewelry of worth in lacs. Gandhiji was free to bring those to India but he made a trust out of entire gifts he had received during his stay in South Africa from 1896 to 1901. The motto of the trust was to serve the cause of the Indians there. When Gandhiji returned from South Africa after 5 years of his stay, this country was experiencing a new era of movements and revolution.

There had been many incidents in the life of Gandhiji which established his policy of maintaining transparency in public life. Because he was well aware of the fact that being an associate of the trade of public life it was just like walking on the razor. When the public servant prompts for praise, why has he to hide his face at the time of criticism? That is why he had once said, "I have concluded that it is prohibited for the public servant to accept any gift."

Gandhiji always felt that people visualized God in their ideals. That is why we should not hurt the public sentiment at any cost. Through his own life he had characterized a ideal public servant and presented it before the Indians who was in love with the people and kept a lot of compassion for them. Any kind of greed was not able to even touch him. Gandhiji always maintained transparency throughout his life and remained blameless.

Maintenance of Account

"Gandhiji was habitual of keeping the accounts accurate since childhood. Since his childhood he was aware of his expenditures and always tried to keep it below 15 pounds during his student life. He used to keep account of the bus fares and postal cost and always checked his cash before going to sleep. This habit remained with him till the end. And he believed that because of this he was able to maintain the account of the transaction of lacs of rupees and used money in the most efficient way and was never compelled to borrow debts for the movements. On the contrary, money was saved after the movements."

Gandhiji was totally aware of the thing that directly or indirectly politics remains in the public life always. Thus there is a need to walk on this path with extra care because whether it is public or personal life of a man the financial transparency is always needed. I have seen many people in my life who earn a lot but their inability to keep accounts of that ruins them at the end. For a successful management employee it is important to be aware of all his accounts. He must be well aware of the status of everything. Gandhiji led a lot of movements during his life time for which he had to collect funds. During these collections many a time he faced adverse situations. Mentioning his experiences in this context Gandhiji said, "Since the very beginning I learnt that debts should be avoided for the public works. People should be trusted for their words but not in the matter of money.

Gandhiji believed that those who do not know the laws and do not follow those are not eligible to be a public servant. He warned a group of politicians who had come for his blessings, "Stay away of power. Power makes the man corrupt. Do not get trapped in the glamour of power. Remember you have been awarded this post to serve the people of the villages of India."

Utilization of the available money in the best possible manner is the requirement for being a successful management employee. He should invest in those areas from which he can earn most profit. He can earn profit for his firm or organization through using money in the best possible way.

For this, the balance between expenditure and earning should be maintained. In this regard, Gandhiji said, "If you want to fulfill your desired aim, you need to learn the art of managing things within your income. There are two ways to accomplish it. First, minimize your necessities and second, do your work in such a way that you avoid debts."

Through his policies, Gandhiji emphasized that along with transparency in public life the strict balance between expenditure and earning is mandatory. He was of the opinion that money should be utilized wisely and transactions of account must be clear. Let us come and implement following principles in life:

- Make your working style and personality transparent.
- Keep your accounts clear.
- Make a habit of checking your balance daily.

❑

16

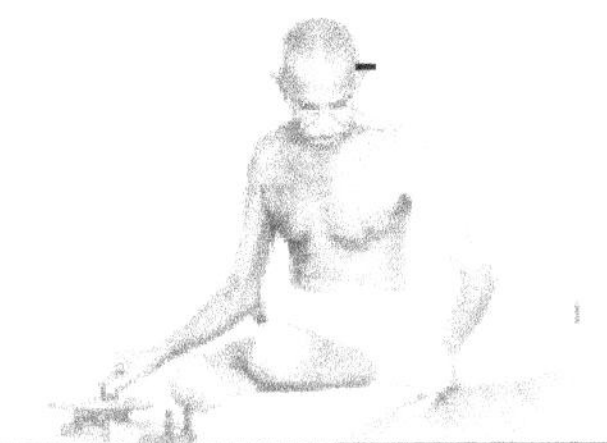

Prepare Right Background

When higher caste Hindus asked me in arrogance, "Will harijans stop drinking liquor, eating the meat of dead, being dirty and other habits? This makes me impatient. Consider if my father, mother, son or daughter is suffering from leprosy then can I say that I will touch them only when they will be completely treated? If I do not serve them at this time I will ridicule the holy relation between them and me."

–Sampurn Gandhi Wangmay (Section-63), Page 43

Preparing the Right Background

Be so firm that any kind of disturbance can not violate your peace of mind. Talk about good health, development and happiness whosoever you meet. Realize your friends that they are worthy. Look at the good part of everything. Think about the best, put your effort for the best and expect the best. Meet everybody with a smiling face. Provide so much of time for your betterment that you will not be able to think about others' drawbacks even for a moment. Be aloof of worry and broaden your thinking that you may never get angry.

To imbibe these qualities it is needed to analyze the situation properly and draw a clear background. There is always a possibility of diversion if you have not drawn the background properly. Before saying anything Gandhiji used to test that on the touchstone of logic and experience and then presented it in an ideal background. Before criticizing the British government he always prepared a proper background on the topic. Then he presented it as an ideal. Commenting on the condition of Indian people during the regime of British government Gandhiji said, "A developed nation has met a underdeveloped nation, so it is the duty of the developed nation to develop the other one. Similarly the king is not the boss or the servant of the people. Officers are not to exert their officialdom but to serve the people. If there are selfish people in the republic then it is of no worth."

It is important for a management employee to have logic and prepare a clear background to prove his point so that even his opponents should agree with him.

In Favour of Economic Equality

Through his policies Gandhiji has always emphasized equality. He wanted to bring not only the political freedom but also the social freedom too. He emphasized that he wanted to establish a society of the kind where there would not be any differentiation. He urged the wealthy people of the nation that they should come forward to support the poor people of the country. That is why he had said also, "As long as this difference of being wealthy and poor will remain, it can be said that we are committing theft."

Gandhiji was totally aware of the fact that at that time it was very important to develop the villages for the welfare of India. Regarding modernization he had said that if it harmed the interests of the workers of the village then it was necessary to be careful and this should be adopted after a clear understanding of it. He always laid an emphasis on the promotion of small scale industries in the villages for its development. He said, "Children should be taught crafts skill and through this their body, mind and soul should be taught. During the course of teaching them this craftsmanship, teachers should highlight the qualities of these children. Children have to be taught math, geography and history. They all are related to this craftsmanship."

Gandhiji said that making soap, paper, match box, leather, refinery, and other manual works should be developed in the villages because in absence of these the development of village would remain a dream. He emphasized that such industries should be promoted in the village area in which there was lesser need of money but more need of labour, so that the poor might get livelihood. He had said, "I do not like wealth accumulated in the hands of few, it should be evenly distributed. The machines of this era helps in making few wealthy. The motive behind it is the greed not the development. This is against my principles for which I am fighting with my full power."

Welfare of Women

Gandhiji knew that for the realization of the dream of freedom it was important to be acknowledged at the societal level of which the women are important part. He also felt that the two classes of the society, women and untouchables, had been marginalized by the evil laws of the society. The entire nation was moving forward and we still are trapped in the superstition and suffocating traditions. Girls were not allowed to attend school or to take part in the development of the society. From child marriage to the sati pratha all these laws had put the entire women of the nation into inertia. That is why he believed that instead of being their friend or colleague male had become their bosses. This is the prime duty of the congreessmen that they strive to elevate the position of women in the society. Gandhiji had said in this regard , "Women are the images of renounce, non-violence, and kindness. Where few people understand non-violence and religion through their intellect, women know it since childhood. Men perform few duties and become content where these sisters have to take care of their husbands, children and other members of the family."

Gandhiji not only emphasized the need for the development of women but also the thing that they should be realized their other responsibilities too. He was of the opinion that Indian women were not like the women of the other part of the world, but they were different in abilities and form. Their role can provide better guidance to the society. In the context of women power he said, "If women has destructive powers the power of creation is inherent in them. This is my desire that they should understand this power of them. If they stop thinking that they are weak and only eligible to be puppets in the hands of male, she can make her life along with the life of her father, child or husband more worthy."

In the above sentence, the art of drawing perfect background is evident. Whenever we want to inspire someone for a cause it is needed to make him understand the goal mentally. It is very much needed to draw a clear background for this. It is also important for a successful management guru to be efficient in this art of making clear background so that he may reach to his good easily.

Keeping all Together

I have said ealier that it is very important for a successful management guru to develop the quality to keep all together for the fulfillment of the aim. For this he has to prepare himself. They will not be respected until they respect others. Without developing the humane qualities none can be respected in the society. I believe that there are two types of human being in the society. There are few people who react immediately as per their behavior. And on the contrary, there are people who do not react but learn for their future. If you want to become a successful management guru you need to develop certain qualities that enables you to be worthy enough to inspire others and there will be a constant increase in the number of the fans. I feel there is rarely anyone in the society who have no enemy. This is not so important to have enemies but the important thing is that whether you are making more friends or enemies by your activities. If 90% people support your policies then you should try to change the remaining 10% as per your policies at their mental level. Gandhiji always emphasized this point. He had said that we should behave in the same way as we expect from others, " I cannot live in this struggling enviornment all around me as long as accept this situation that all religions are same and there is same respect for other religions within me as for my own religion."

Effort to Maintain Compassion in the Advesre Situations

Gandhiji has said,"Those are selfish who long only for the betterment of himself or his caste.

In the light of the above statement, you can understand his mentality and his efforts at the time of partition. He always tried to learn from his experience and time. Once someone said to him on few subjects you had opined differently at different places. Replying this, Gandhiji said that he always tried to learn new things. And in course of this whenever I felt that I had mistaken I promptly rectify that. Because during this course of learning I had learn a lot. Describing his passion for learning he said if everybody would become the teacher who would the student? So we should be the students. He not only said this but followed as well. Whenever he got a chance to learn new things he leant those and applied in his life if deemed fit. This is also true for a management guru. He should be teacher as well as student. He should act as teacher in others'views and be a student to learn new things always. A consistency in this effort can bring ideal background.

When the fire of riots were soaring high on both parts, India and Pakistan, few tried to put some oil in the fire. At that time also Gandhiji tried to maintain peace on both sides. Anyhow the feeling of love, brotherhood, peace and friendly environment should be restored again. To eliminate the hatred of both sides he gave a message and requested the people," "If we remember the fact that life is one then there will not be any reason for this violence. Every Hindu should try to read Quaran, Muslim should understand Vedas, Geeta and the Guru granth Sahib of Sikhs. We should respect the others' religion in the same way as we do ours. It does not matter which language has been used be it Sanskrit or Arabic but the truth will remain always truth."

It is important for any management guru to draw a clear background before establishing any policy. And then present it in an appropriate environment so that it may be appreciated as well as understood widely. Gandhiji always kept in mind that before going for something the background must be prepared properly. Let us imbibe following qualities of Gandhiji in our lives:

- Prepare a proper background before implementing any policy.
- Get help from required people.
- Inspire all to perform at their best.
- Be compassionate with colleague.

❑

17

Health Awareness

I have believed and I still believe that we should manage time for exercise as we manage time for eating. It does not matter how busy the schedule is. In my humble opinion, this will increase the service for the nation.

–My Experiments with Truth, P 225.

Health Awareness

It is of no worth that a human being earns lot of money but at the cost of his health and family. Today there is lust for money across the world, in consequence a lot of people are working only for money. They want to earn as much as possible at any cost. They are willing to pay any cost for it. But this is not good. If a man earns a lot but is not in a position to utilize that, what is worth earning so much of money? During my life I have seen many people who have lost their health for money and ultimately they were unable to recover lost things.

A philosopher has said that God gives the share of food to the beggars to whom he provides golden plates. There are so many people in our society who have huge sum of wealth and resources but their body is not in a condition to enjoy that. So, no matter in which field we work, the important thing is to be aware of health. Gandhiji is an ideal in this field. He always tried to maintain his routine. He consistently avoided things which were harmful for his health. Whenever someone starts remaining busy in public work, the daily routine starts disorganizing. But you can't defend yourself by saying that what can you do, your routine is like that. If you wish, you can maintain your health and routine in any condition or environment. In this context, Gandhiji had said, "I have believed and still believe that as we manage time for food, we can manage time for exercise. In my humble opinion this will increase the service to nation instead of decreasing it".

Emphasis on Using Appropriate Resources

It is important for a successful management guru to inspire others to perform at their best, along with it he should also follow the rules himself which enables him to be fit.

There was acute shortage of modern facilities of healthcare and medicine before independence. Across the nation, so many epidemics spread time and again. These cost millions of lives. Gandhiji emphasized the need to lower down the death rate and to launch a campaign of health awareness. He said, "Definitely, the reason of high death rate is poverty which is damaging the body of the countrymen. But if they are taught about the tips of being fit and healthy, this can be lowered down. When got ill, treat it with the available natural resources".

The Magic of Will Power

The biggest power Gandhiji had had his "will power". He strived to do at any cost whatever he once determined to do. There are so many incidents in the life of Gandhiji which explains his health awareness. Once Kasturba fell ill seriously. Gandhiji used all his knowledge of medicine but nothing happened. Then a doctor advised that if 'Bao' stopped consuming salt and pulse, there would be definite improvement. Gandhiji said to Kasturba to stop consuming pulse and salt, this would help you in recovering. Kasturba said you say whatever you like. Consider for once how difficult it is to stop consuming pulse and salt? Gandhiji replied that if you were thinking like that then I would also stop consuming pulse and salt. Later, Kasturba urged him to take back his words. He replied, "I can't take back my promise. I will be in profit. If man follows any kind of control for any purpose, it is always beneficial."

It is important for any management Guru to strictly follow the health guidelines and inspire others to do the same in all circumstances. There is a need to develop will power for this within yourself. We should not consume those things that are injurious to our health. Along with this positive attitude, happiness, and regular exercise enhance physical abilities. Gandhiji has perfectly exemplified this at various plans during his life. We should implement following things from today onwards drawing inspirations from him: –

- Be aware about your health.
- Maintain a balanced diet and routine.
- Do not forget exercise ever.
- Do not let your will power die.

❑

18

Development of Spiritual Consciousness

I am humble servant of truth. I am eager to gain self-knowledge. I want salvation (Moksha) in this life. My service to my country is Spiritualism through which I want to free get myself from the bondage of birth. I do not long for the mortal state of the world. I am striving for that heaven that is called 'Mukti' (liberation). For achieving my goal, I do not need to go into a cave. The cave is within me, if I am able to know that.

Young India, 3-4-1924

Development of Spiritual Consciousness

Gandhiji studied various sacred scriptures like the Geeta, Ramayana, Quran, Bible etc. during his lifetime. He learnt the theory of karma from Geeta and Upanishads. There was a deep influence of those scriptures on Gandhiji's behaviour, thinking and philosophy. Because of this influence Gandhiji followed the path of truth, non-violence and satyagrah during his life time.

The feeling of renounce was developed within him because of these holy books. Gandhiji had himself said, "I consider Geeta unmatched for its philosophy of truth". One has the right to work, he has not the right to results". After understanding Mahatma Gandhi you can understand that *'Bhagwat Geeta'* had deep impact on Gandhiji". He not only studied *Geeta*, but also adopted its teachings into his life.

Gandhiji was influenced with the ideas and teachings of Jesus. He learnt from it that evil by good, hate by love, violence by non-violence and enemy by friendship could be won.

Gandhiji was also influenced by Gautam Buddha. That's why he adopted the path of kindness, love and non-violence. Great philosopher Leo Tolstoy's works like *"Live and Let Live"* and *"The Kingdom of God is Within You"* helped Gandhiji to become a spiritual man. There was a deep impact on the life of Mahatama Gandhi of Tolstoy. Gandhiji considered himself the disciple of Tolstoy. He had said, "Tolstoy is one of the three persons who has influenced my life very much".

Value of Love

Gandhiji did not ever use harsh and uncultured words even against his opponents. Because he considered them also the son of the Almighty. He believed that to love one who loved you was easy but we were really tested when we started loving someone who hated you. This is easy to hear or read it. But it is quite hard to implement in life. When General Dyre ordered to kill thousands of people in 'Jaliawala Bagh', at that time Gandhiji had said that I prayed God to give some sense to the people like Dyre. At first these words may seem unusual, but when you ponder deeply on it, it can be felt that one cannot say these words until his soul is enlightened and he is spiritual. There was a great soul within , which had so fastly broadened to understand the philosophy of Gandhiji. One need to broaden his understanding and thinking to understand Gandhi. Once he had said, "It is not non-violence to love those who love you. Actually non-violence is to love those who hate you. I know how difficult it is to follow rules of love. But it is hard to implement good and great philosophy. It is very tough to love one who hates you. But if we are all eager to do then the most difficult ones are possible with the grace of God".

Motto of Life

Gandhiji believed that all the living organisms are the part of same God. That's why he opposed untouchability, and difference in the society. Gandhiji had said if there is the same God in all then how could people be different on the basis of caste and religion? He made service an instrument to get to the goal. He believed that by serving the poor he serves God. He not only said these words but also followed it. He said, "The motto of my life is definitely to enjoy to know ourself and our soul. We cannot know our soul until we learn to unite with all. So, it is important for us to know the God residing within all. And this knowledge can be gained through selfless service only".

Thinking About Religion

"All religions are just like different path that lead to the same destination. If these lead us to our goal, then what is the impact of being those different? Actually there are as many religions as human beings. As long as there are different religions, each religion needs an external symbol but when that external symbol becomes only hypocrisy and that is used to establish the Supremacy of a particular religion over others, it becomes renounced".

The above statement of Gandhiji proves that he emphasized the need to respect each religion equally. He believed that there was no humanism within, it was impossible to follow the path of religion. He said that our respect for other religions would earn respect for our religion too. All religions have different paths and all have to reach the same destination i.e. the Almighty. So, it is against morality to criticize or oppose other religion. For this we need the help of policy. That policy should be made for the welfare of all. He has said, "Religion cannot survive in the absence of policy. True policy imbibes a lot from religion. Those who follow the rules not for selfishness but for the policy, can be called religious".

Following are the views of Gandhiji regarding religion:

- All religions have different paths that lead to same destination. If we are moving in the same direction, then what is the harm in following different paths.
- That does not care for practical matters is not a religion.
- Religion is tested at the time of adversity.
- Religion saves man in the adverse situation.
- Those who are taught religion since childhood, devotion, faith etc. develop in their behaviour.

- Religion is a bridge to reach God.
- The biggest religion is to know our soul. The religion cannot be abandoned even at the cost of wealth, respect, relatives and life.
- Man without religion is just like a boat without oar.

Faith in God

Gandhiji has said that truth is a kind of godly power or it can be said, "Truth is God". Believing in God and Hinduism he always opposed untouchability. This was his biggest power. Gandhiji accepted humanism as his religion. He said that religion was taught us to perform our duties. And this is not implacable on the people only but on the rulers too. Gandhiji used Satyagrah as a powerful weapon. He had turned the table in his favour many a time on the basis of silence and fast. His ashram was not only a spiritual centre. But also social service, how to educate illiterates, primary education, and the methods to abolish violence, difference and untouchability were taught there.

Gandhiji had firm faith in God. That is why, his internal spiritualism was ever growing. When you have firm faith in God, you are saved from so many unwanted things. Along with this, it is source of energy for your soul at the time of crises. Gandhiji himself has said, "The root of all mental evils are same and that is non-acceptance of God. Repeating the name of God or going to pilgrimage. This should be matter of soul and those who have insisted it in hearts need nothing to get satisfied. Those are winners who have satisfied God and those who haven't done it are losers even after satisfying thousands because to satisfy each human being one has to lose itself".

Gandhiji believed that truth is a way to reach God. It may be possible that for time being it may seem bad but the truth must be accepted with all its bitterness. He believed that truth and love cannot be destroyed ever. You can not destroy it with the means of fear and violence. That's why he said, "I can say you this that I believe more in God than the fact that you and we are sitting in this room. I can also say that I can survive without God. Snatch my eyes I will be still alive. Cut my nose, it can force me to die. But if you draw out my faith in God, I will die at that moment. You may say it superstition, but I accept it from the purest of my Soul that this is superstition that I have embraced lovingly".

Gandhian philosophy lays emphasis on spiritual aspect. Gandhiji got inspiration from Socrates. Socrates was the first in the world who consumed poison for the sake of truth. This incident influenced Gandhiji. Similarly, the thoughts of Henry David also inspired Gandhiji. The idea of Satyagrah was drawn from him by Gandhiji. Gandhiji also got the inspiration after the policies of co-operation and non-co-operation from 'Thoro'.

Following are the ideas of Gandhiji regarding faith in God.

- Those who forget God, forget himself.
- There must be result of the words that come out of purest of the heart.
- One does so many exercises to save the body, does it strive similarly for knowing the soul?
- The true light comes out from inside.
- God resides in each soul and thus each soul is a temple.
- If God resides in each soul, whom we disrespect?
- The external peace is of no worth in absence of internal peace.
- Those who keep talking about their sorrow multiplies it all the more.

- We are not able to do anything until we get light from within.
- If the soul enlightened there is light all around.
- Those who do not have peace and firmness, can't reach to God.
- Never suppress your inner voice even though you are alone.
- Human being develops as much as it gets closer to soul.
- The real coward is within not outside.

Gandhiji always utilized his time to its fullest. With the help of spiritualism, he had developed sheer power of determination and self-confidence within. And because of this he never lost his patience. If management employee develops spiritual conscience within, it helps him to enhance his abilities and self-confidence. So, apply following things in your life right from today:

- Believe in God.
- Do not panic in adverse situations.
- Try your best to achieve your goal, be composed even though you fail. Try again.
- Perform your job with pure soul and total ability. Have faith in God. Those who do things with pure heart are supported by God.

❑

19

Acceptability of Own Mistakes

"Yesterday I criticized Tyagiji. He is angry. I have committed a blunder that without examining the facts I perceived that true. I beg pardon for that. We all should vow that we will not reach to the conclusion without examining the facts. This is my penance for the mistake."

–Mahatma Gandhi

Acceptability of Own Mistakes

Whenever we commit a mistake we should accept those without any hesitation. When I commit mistakes I must have the courage to change myself. And when I do something good I must have the humbleness so that I cannot be an arrogant and people can stay with me comfortably. This is the best to live life. Gandhiji is remembered as the best example for this philosophy. He always learnt from his mistakes. He never hesitated to accept his mistakes. He had many a time accepted his mistakes before the people and observed penance for that. In this context he had said:

- Because of penance the feeling of renounce develops within for the earlier mistakes and it makes us aware for the future.
- Penance should come out of heart.
- Those who observe penance from the heart are worthy of compassion.
- The feeling of penance should come out of one's own heart and along with that it should be vowed that this will not be repeated.
- Penance should be observed only when the mistake was committed unknowingly.

Once Gandhiji being angry criticized one of his disciples publically. But later when he know the facts , he felt that there was no any mistake of his disciple, Tyagiji. He begged pardon publically and said,

"Yesterday I criticized Tyagiji. He is angry. I have committed a blunder that without examining the facts I considered those right. I beg pardon for that. We should decide that we will never reach to conclusion without examining the facts. This is penance for my mistake."

A management employee should be so flexible that he can accept his mistakes without any hesitation. This brings maturity in his personality and people will praise him.

Acceptance of Weaknesses

This is important for a management guru that he should review his personality, previous works, policies etc. If he is able to do so he will be able to cast out vices within himself. If he does not review, he will keep committing mistakes and this can hamper the prospect of getting to the aim. Gandhiji never hide his mistakes on the contrary he accepted and tried to rectify those. This acceptance of mistake provided him a source of energy. Instaed of being weak at adverse times, he came out strongly. In the context of accepting mistakes before others Gandhiji said, " I leant not to repeat mistakes from the acceptance of it before others. None can hide his misdeeds. When God can see those misdeeds why can't he? Those who are ashamed of their mistakes will be safe after revealing it and can make his friends his guards in this matter. This can be considered as being dependent on God. I should accept that. Many a time, I had been saved from committing mistakes and this happened because of my wife, children and friends.

Once Gandhiji was going to Johhanesburg during his stay in South Africa. He had the ticket of horse's 'sirkam'. He had written in his autobiography that every traveller had to sit inside the sirkam, but I was a coolie and the owner of the sirkam provided me seat to sit with the driver so that I may not sit with white people inside. The white sitting inside asked him to sit at their feet. Gandhiji opposed that and said, 'You made me sit here but I did not utter a word. I had the ticket to sit inside, but you made me to sit here outside. Now I am ready to sit inside but am not going to sit at your feet.' Hardly I realized that there were rain of slapping on me and the white were forcing me outside. I grabbed the bronze chain hanging there and vowed not to leave that at any cost. He was cursing me, pulling me and beating me. I was tolerating all that silently. He was powerful and I was powerless."

Gandhiji never tried to hide his shortcomings and those feeling with whom he was not agree with. Even once I have committed the mistake to beat the child but I oppose this. Accepting his mistake he notes in his biography, " I have always been against the beating of the child. I remember only one occasion when I beat one of my sons. I was right or wrong, I have not been able to adjudge that."

Other Examples of Acceptance

Once Gandhiji asked Kasturba to do something as per his principles and when 'Ba' denied, Gandhiji begging pardon said, "This is my mistake that I am not able to convince you of my principles. I am the sinner."

Gandhiji always tried to finish his tasks in less possible time. His knowledge was based on his experience. He had gained broad knowledge through books , but he was not satisfied with his knowledge. He wanted to read more books on different issues. Accepting this desire he said, "After entering into the field of work there is less time. So, even today it can be said that my bookish knowledge is very less."

In context of his mistakes following are his ideas:

- Accepting mistakes is like sweeping. It clears the dirt and makes the floor clean.
- Nature has created us in such a way that we can not see our back and only others can see it. So we should get benefit of others.
- Do not commit this blunder to consider yourself perfect.
- Accepting mistakes is beneficial.

- Every body commits mistakes. Accepting the mistake or vice as soon they are known means casting them out of yourself.
- Everybody commits mistake but it becomes dangerous when one tries to hide it.
- Mistakes can not be defended through the means of logic. Sacred scriptures across the world can't defend those.
- Man learns from their mistakes but does not provide you a license to commit mistakes forever.
- If human being rectifies those mistakes he can move forward with cautious steps.

For being a successful management guru it is required to rectify your mistakes as soon as possible. Learning from those mistakes he should draw future policies in such a way that these should not be repeated ever. Gandhiji was an ideal in this context. He not only accepted his mistakes but also observed penance if he deemed it fit. Before preaching others we need to follow those ourselves and we should present us as an ideal.

We should accept our mistakes without any hesitation. In this context Gandhiji had said, "There are few who are ashamed of accepting their mistakes and few try to hide those. But the religion says all the time visualise the tiny vices as single piece of rice as the mountain , if you accept those from your heart then you will be clean in the same way as the clothes get clean after wash. And you will be even pure. Acceptance of the mistake publically and observing penance will serve as a protection against vices in the future." From this chapter what we learn, we should implement following things in our lives:

- Remain always aware of your duties.
- Do not consider any job inferior.

- Change your life style if required for the achievement of the goal.
- Set examples for others through your duty.

There is none in this world who has achieved success in their life without experience and experiments. For achieving success, constant efforts, labour, studies and new experiments with self-analysis is required . That is why, a successful management guru should analyse things without any presumption. After reading this book and understanding Gandhiji's ideology you must have been feeling that he still can guide our management skills and give a new direction to it. Drawing inspiration from him we must start transforming ourselves.

❑

About The Author

Name	: Praveen Shukla
Date of Birth	: June 7, 1970
Birth Place	: Pilkhuwa, Ghaziabad, U.p.
Education qualification	: M.A. (Economics, Hindi), B.Ed.
Other Achievements	: Popularised Through Akashwani, Times F.M., Doordarsan, Zee TV, NDTV, Sahara TV, SAB TV, and other channels.

Honours And Awards

1. 'Kavya Ganga Award' 1993, Hapur, U.P.
2. 'Vyang Shree Award' 1998, Bharatpur, Rajasthan
3. 'Hindi Gaurav Award' 1998,Delhi
4. 'Shreshth Kavi Award' 1999, Jabalpur, M.p.
5. 'Parsone Smriti Award' 2003, Bhopal, M.P.
6. 'Sharda Award' 2003, Ghaziabad, U.P.
7. 'Attahas Yuva Rachnakar Award', 2004, Lucknow,U.P,
8. 'Shresth Hindi Sevi Award'2004, Lions Club, Delhi Prabhat
9. 'Kavya Hansh Samman' 2006, Lions Club, Model Town, Delhi
10. 'Omprakash Aditya Award' 2006, Delhi
11. 'Dr. Urmilesh Shankhdhar Award', 2007, Lucknow,U.P.
12. 'Mr. Mast Award', 2009, Delhi
13. 'Kavya Gaurav Award', 2009, Dehradun (Prize Money 1 Lac)

Creative Work

1. *'Swar Ehsanso Ke'* , Amrit Prakashan,Delhi
2. *'Kahan We Kahan Ye'* , Diamond Books, Delhi
3. *'Hanste Hansate Raho'*, Diamond Books,Delhi

Song Collections

1. *Tumhari Aankh Ke Aansu,* Diamond Books, Delhi

Prose Collections

Gandhi Aur Gandhigiri, Diamond Books, (Translated in Gujarati, Marathi and English)

Travelogues

Safar Badlon Ka, Diamond Books, Delhi

Edited Works

1. *Har Hal Main Khush Hai* (Popular Poems Of Alhar Bikaneri)
2. *Ek Pyar Ka Nagma Hai* (Popular Songs Of Santoshnand)
3. *Muhabbat Hai Kya Chiz* (Popular Songs Of Santoshnand)

Audio CD

Na Wo Sawan Raha (popular Songs of Praveen Shukla)

Published Creations

1. *Dr. Ashok Chakradhar Ke Kayvya Main Vyang Chetana,* Research Paper
2. *Aaina Achha Laga,* Gazal Collections
3. *Netaji Ka Chunawi Daura,* Collection of humours stories

Columns

He writes Satire regularly in leading newspapers like *Punjab Keshri, Dainik Hindustan, Navbharat Times, Hari Bhumi* and *Many* more.

Foreign Tours

Bankok, Dubai, many cities of U.K. (London, Burmingham, Nautingham, Yorkshire, Manchester etc.)

Special

He has been a regular invitee of many literary programmes across the country. So far more than 1000 *Kavi Sammelans* has been attended by him along with many other programmes where he was the anchor. He has been part of prestigious Lal *Kila Kavi Sammelan, Swatantrata Diwas Kavi Sammelan, Janta Ki Pukar Kavi Sammelan, DCM Kavi Sammelan* and many more.

Profession : Professor (Economics)

Address: 4649/15-A, New Modern Sahadara, Delhi,110032

Tele. No.- (011) 22111464, M.n.-(0)9312600362

Email : kavipraveenshukla@rediffmail.com

Website: kavisamelan.com, praveensukla.com

SELF HELP

Walking with you in the shades of Love
Deepak Yadav

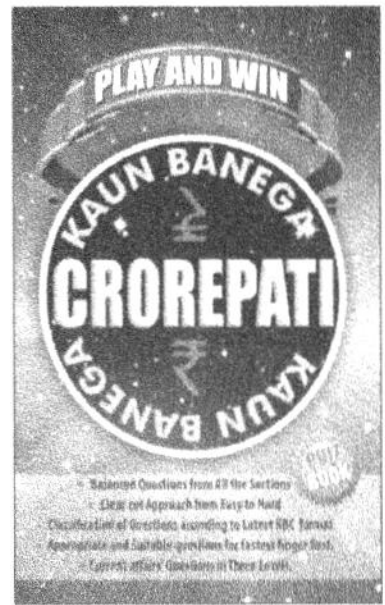
PLAY AND WIN
KAUN BANEGA CROREPATI KAUN BANEGA

POWER THINKING
Dr. Ujjwal Patni

YOUR MONEY MY ADVICE
Practical Money Making Ideas for Complete Financial Freedom
Subhash Lakhotia

GOLDEN KEY TO BECOME SUPER RICH
Subhash Lakhotia

STOP LOSING
START WINNING
ASHU DUTT

DR. BIMAL CHHAJER
201 TIPS FOR GAS OR ACIDITY
Get Rid of Gas or Acidity a disease of Modern Busy Life

gandhi and management

SECRETS OF SUCCESS THROUGH BHAGWAD GEETA
AUTHORS NAME

SECRETS OF SUCCESS

No.1 Bestseller
Learn to Say NO if You don't Want to Say Yes

Subhash Lakhotia
Secrets of Super Success

Jolly Uncle
Stories that Enlighten You
JPS Jolly

TIPS OF SUCCESS
Dr. Sunil Joat

PERFECT SUCCESS Mantras

Aim High For Bigger WIN
Tarun Engineer

www.ingramcontent.com/pod-product-compliance
Ingram Content Group UK Ltd.
Pitfield, Milton Keynes, MK11 3LW, UK
UKHW021658190726
13853UKWH00001B/336

9 788128 827587